CONTENTS

THIRD EDITION

An Introduction to Multicultural Education

James A. Banks
University of Washington, Seattle

Allyn and Bacon
Boston ▪ London ▪ Toronto ▪ Sydney ▪ Tokyo ▪ Singapore

Editor in Chief: *Paul A. Smith*
Series Editor: *Traci Mueller*
Editorial Assistant: *Bridget Keane*
Marketing Manager: *Amy Cronin*
Editorial-Production Service: *Chestnut Hill Enterprises, Inc.*
Manufacturing Buyer: *Suzanne Lareau*
Cover Administrator: *Kristina Mose-Libon*
Electronic Composition: *Omegatype Typography, Inc.*

A Pearson Education Company
75 Arlington Street
Boston, MA 02116

Internet: www.ablongman.com

Between the time Website information is gathered and then published, it is not unusual for some sites to have closed. Also, the transcription of URLs can result in unintended typographical errors. The publisher would appreciate notification where these occur so that they may be corrected in subsequent editions.

Credits are found on page 163, which should be considered an extension of the copyright page.

Library of Congress Cataloging-in-Publication Data

Banks, James A.
An introduction to multicultural education / James A. Banks. — 3rd ed.
p. cm.
Includes bibliographical references and index.
ISBN 0-205-34102-0
1. Multicultural education—United States.

LC1099.3 .B36 2002
370.117—dc21

2001046132

Printed in the United States of America

10 9 8 7 6 5 4 3 2 1 06 05 04 03 02 01

To
Angela and Patricia, my children
to whom the torch will pass

An Introduction to Multicultural Education

PREFACE

As our nation's ethnic texture continues to deepen, the challenge of educating students to function effectively in a pluralistic society intensifies. More than one-third of the students in the nation's public elementary and secondary schools are students of color. Students of color will make up nearly one-half of all students in the United States by the end of the second decade of this century. The percentage of these who speak a first language other than English is also increasing. About 14 percent of the nation's school-age youth speak a first language other than English. The gap between the rich and the poor is also widening within our society. Nearly one of every five students is a victim of poverty.

The increasing racial, ethnic, and language diversity within the United States presents both challenges and opportunities. To respond effectively, teachers and administrators need to have a sophisticated grasp of the concepts, principles, theories, and practices in multicultural education. They also need to examine and clarify their own racial and ethnic attitudes and to develop the pedagogical knowledge and skills needed to work effectively with students from diverse cultural, racial, ethnic, language, and social-class groups.

An Introduction to Multicultural Education, Third Edition, is designed to introduce preservice and practicing educators to the major concepts, principles, theories, and practices in multicultural education. It was written for readers who can devote only limited time to the topic. Chapter 1 discusses the goals of multicultural education and the widespread misconceptions about it. The dimensions of multicultural education and the characteristics of an effective multicultural school are discussed in Chapter 2. Chapter 3 describes the ways in which multicultural education seeks to transform the curriculum so that all students will acquire the knowledge, attitudes, and skills needed to become effective citizens in a pluralistic democratic society. The idea that multicultural education is in the nation's shared public interest is a key tenet of this chapter.

School reform and intergroup education are discussed in Chapter 4. The need to reform the nation's schools in order to respond to its demographic changes is examined in the first part; the second part discusses intergroup education and the nature of students' racial attitudes. Guidelines for helping students develop more positive racial attitudes and values are presented. School reform with goals related to both increasing academic achievement and helping students to develop more positive racial attitudes are essential if the United States is to compete effectively in an interdependent global society and help all students to become caring, committed, and active citizens.

The knowledge components needed by practicing educators to function effectively in multicultural classrooms and schools are examined in Chapters 5 and 6. The types of knowledge effective teachers need are described in Chapter 5. This chapter also describes the major paradigms, key concepts, and powerful ideas, as well as the kinds of historical and cultural knowledge related to ethnic groups needed by today's educators. Chapter 6 discusses the characteristics of multicultural lessons and units that are organized around powerful ideas and concepts. It contains two teaching units that exemplify these characteristics.

The goals of citizen education in a multicultural society are discussed in Chapter 7. This chapter also describes the ways in which I help teachers to examine and reconstruct the mainstream American metanarrative in one of my teacher education courses at the University of Washington. In the interview that constitutes Chapter 8, some of the concepts and issues discussed in previous chapters are revisited and clarified. Chapter 9 summarizes the book with a discussion of major benchmarks that educators can use to determine whether a school or educational institution is implementing multicultural education in its best and deepest sense.

In preparing this Third Edition of *An Introduction to Multicultural Education,* I have incorporated new developments, trends, and issues throughout the text. I have also updated the references throughout the book. Chapter 8, as well as Appendixes A and E, are new to this edition.

This book was written to provide readers with a brief, comprehensive overview of multicultural education, a grasp of its complexity, and a helpful understanding of what it means for educational practice. Readers who want to study multicultural education in greater depth will find the references at the end of the book—as well as Appendix E, which consists of *A Basic Multicultural Education Library*—helpful resources. I hope this book will start readers on an enriching path in multicultural education that will continue and deepen throughout their careers.

Acknowledgments

I thank Cherry A. McGee Banks for being a colleague and friend who always listens and responds with thoughtful and keen insights. I am grateful to Margaret Smith Crocco for inviting me to do the interview that constitutes Chapter 8 while I was at Teachers College, Columbia University giving the Sachs lectures. I thank my colleagues in the College of Education and the Center for Multicultural Education—especially Geneva Gay, Michael S. Knapp, Walter C. Parker, and Tom Stritikus—for stimulating conversations about race, class, diversity, language, and education. These colleagues help to make the College and the Center rich intellectual communities. The following reviewers offered helpful suggestions: Tonya Huber, Wichita State University; Lucretia Peebles, Spelman College; Evelyn M. Reid, University of Toledo; and Johnnie Thompson, Wichita State University.

J. A. B.

CHAPTER 1 Goals and Misconceptions

Multicultural education is a reform movement designed to make some major changes in the education of students. Multicultural education theorists and researchers believe that many school, college, and university practices related to race and ethnicity are harmful to students and reinforce many of the ethnic stereotypes and discriminatory practices in U.S. society.

Multicultural education assumes that race, ethnicity, culture, and social class are salient parts of U.S. society. It also assumes that ethnic and cultural diversity enriches the nation and increases the ways in which its citizens can perceive and solve personal and public problems. This diversity also enriches a society by providing all citizens with more opportunities to experience other cultures and thus to become more fulfilled as human beings. When individuals are able to participate in a variety of ethnic cultures, they are more able to benefit from the total human experience.

Goals

The Goals of Multicultural Education

Individuals who know the world only from their own cultural and ethnic perspectives are denied important parts of the human experience and are culturally and ethnically encapsulated. These individuals are also unable to know their own cultures fully because of their ethnic blinders. We can get a full view of our own backgrounds and behaviors only by viewing them from the perspectives of other racial and ethnic cultures. Just as fish are unable to appreciate the uniqueness of their aquatic environment, so are many mainstream American students unable to fully see and appreciate the uniqueness of their cultural characteristics. A key goal of multicultural education is to help individuals gain greater self-understanding by viewing themselves from the perspectives of other cultures. Multicultural education assumes that with acquaintance and understanding, respect may follow.

Another major goal of multicultural education is to provide students with cultural and ethnic alternatives. Historically, the school curriculum has focused primarily on the culture and history of mainstream Anglo Americans. The school culture and curriculum were primarily extensions of the culture of mainstream Anglo American students. The school rarely presented mainstream students with cultural and ethnic alternatives.

The Anglocentric curriculum, which still exists to varying degrees in the nation's schools, colleges, and universities, has harmful consequences for both mainstream Anglo American students and students of color, such as African Americans and Mexican Americans. By teaching mainstream U.S. students only about their own cultures, the school is denying them the richness of the music, literature, values, lifestyles, and perspectives of such ethnic groups as African Americans, Puerto Rican Americans, and Polish Americans. Mainstream American students should know that African American literature is uniquely enriching, and that groups such as Italian Americans and Mexican Americans have values they can embrace.

The Anglocentric curriculum negatively affects many students of color because they often find the school culture alien, hostile, and self-defeating. Because of the negative ways in which students of color and their cultures are often viewed by educators and the negative experiences of these students in their communities and in the schools, many of them do not attain the skills needed to function successfully in a highly technological, knowledge-oriented society (Anyon, 1997; Tharp, Estrada, Dalton, & Yamauchi, 2000).

A major goal of multicultural education is to provide all students with the skills, attitudes, and knowledge needed to function within their ethnic culture, within the mainstream culture, and within and across other ethnic cultures. Mainstream American students should have a sophisticated understanding and appreciation for the uniqueness and richness of Black English (also called Ebonics, which is formed from the words *ebony* and *phonics*). African American students should be able to speak and write standard English and to function successfully within mainstream institutions without experiencing cultural alienation from family and community (Perry & Delpit, 1998). The widespread misunderstandings and misconceptions about Ebonics among Americans within many groups became acutely evident when a controversy about it arose in the Oakland (California) Public Schools during the 1996–97 school year.

Another major goal of multicultural education is to reduce the pain and discrimination that members of some ethnic and racial groups experience because of their unique racial, physical, and cultural characteristics. Filipino Americans, Mexican Americans, Puerto Rican Americans, and Chinese Americans often deny their ethnic identity, ethnic heritage, and family in order to assimilate and to participate more fully in American mainstream institutions. Jewish Americans, Polish Americans, and Italian Americans also frequently reject parts of their ethnic cultures when trying to succeed in school and in mainstream society (Brodkin, 1998; Jacoby, 2000; McGoldrick, Giordano, & Pearce, 1996). As Mildred Dickeman (1973) has insightfully pointed out, schools often force members of these groups to experience "self-alienation" in order to succeed. This is a high price to pay for educational, social, and economic mobility.

Some individuals of color, such as many African Americans, Native Americans, and Puerto Rican Americans, in their effort to assimilate and to participate fully in mainstream institutions, become very Anglo-Saxon in their ways of viewing the world and in their values and behavior. However, highly culturally assimilated members of ethnic groups of color are often denied full participation in mainstream institutions because of their skin color (Cose, 1993; Delgado, 1995; Feagin & Sikes, 1994). These individuals may also become alienated from their ethnic communities and families in their attempts to fully participate in mainstream institutions. They may become alienated from both their ethnic cultures and mainstream society and consequently experience marginality.

Jewish Americans and Italian Americans may also experience "marginality" when they try to deny their ethnic heritages and to become fully assimilated into mainstream Anglo society and culture. Although they can usually succeed in looking and in acting like Anglo Americans, they are likely to experience psychological stress and identity conflict when they deny and reject family and their ethnic languages, symbols, behaviors, and beliefs (Brodkin, 1998). Ethnicity plays a major role in the socialization of many members of ethnic groups; ethnic identity is an important part of the identity of such individuals. When these individuals deny their ethnic cultures and identities, they reject an important part of self.

It is important for educators to realize, however, that for many individual members of ethnic groups, ethnic group membership is not an important part of their personal identity. Other group affiliations, such as religion, social class, gender, or sexual orientation, are much more important identities for these individuals. Some people identify with more than one ethnic group (Heath & McLaughlin, 1993). This is especially likely to be the case for individuals who are racially and ethnically mixed—an increasing population within American society (Nash, 1999; Root, 1996). Ethnic identity becomes complicated for individuals of color for whom ethnic identity is not significant. Even though such individuals may not view their ethnic group membership as important, other people, especially those within other racial and ethnic groups, may view these individuals as members of a racial/ethnic group and think that ethnicity is their primary identity.

Ethnic group members who experience marginality are likely to be alienated citizens who feel that they have little stake in society. Those who reject their basic group identity are incapable of becoming fully functioning and self-actualized citizens and are more likely to experience political and social alienation. It thus is in the best interests of a political democracy to protect the rights of all citizens to maintain allegiances to their ethnic and cultural groups (Kymlicka, 1995). Individuals are capable of maintaining allegiance both to their ethnic group and to the nation-state (Banks, 1997a).

Another goal of multicultural education is to help students to master essential reading, writing, and math skills. Multicultural education assumes that multicultural content can help students to master important skills in these areas. Multicultural readings and data can be highly motivating and meaningful (Graff, 1992; Lee, 1993). Students are more likely to master skills when the teacher uses content that deals with significant human problems, such as race, ethnicity, and social class within U.S. society. All American students live in a society in which ethnic, racial, and cultural problems are real and salient. Content related to race, ethnicity, and culture in U.S. society and to the ethnic and cultural communities in which students live is significant and meaningful to students. Multicultural education theorists and researchers believe that skill goals are extremely important.

Education within a pluralistic society should affirm and help students understand their home and community cultures. However, it should also help free them from their cultural boundaries. To create and maintain a civic community that works for the common good, education in a democratic society should help students acquire the knowledge, attitudes, and skills needed to participate in civic action to make society more equitable and just.

The Multicultural Debate

Multicultural education is an education for freedom that is essential in today's ethnically polarized and troubled world (Parekh, 1986). During the early 1990s it evoked a divisive national debate, in part because of the divergent views that citizens hold about what constitutes an American identity and about the roots and nature of American civilization. In turn, the debate sparked a power struggle over who should participate in formulating the canon used to shape the curriculum in the nation's schools, colleges, and universities (Carnochan, 1993).

The bitter canon debate in the popular press and in several widely reviewed books overshadowed the progress in multicultural education that has been made during the last two decades. The debate also perpetuated harmful misconceptions about theory and practice in multicultural education. It consequently increased racial and ethnic tension and trivialized the field's remarkable accomplishments in theory, research, and curriculum development. The truth about the development and attainments of multicultural education needs to be told, for the sake of balance, scholarly integrity, and accuracy.

Misconceptions

Multicultural Education Is for the Others

To reveal the truth about multicultural education, some of the frequently repeated and widespread myths and misconceptions about it must be identified and debunked. One such misconception is that multicultural education is an entitlement program and curriculum movement for African Americans, Latinos, the poor, women, and other marginalized groups (D'Souza, 1995; Glazer, 1997; Leo, 2000).

The major theorists and researchers in multicultural education agree that it is a reform movement designed to restructure educational institutions so that all students, including White, male, and middle-class students, will acquire the knowledge, skills, and attitudes needed to function effectively in a culturally and ethnically diverse nation and world (Banks, 2001; Banks & Banks, 1995; Gay, 1995; Grant & Sleeter, 2001). Multicultural education, as defined and conceptualized by its major architects during the last decade, is not an ethnic- or gender-specific movement, but a movement designed to empower all students to become knowledgeable, caring, and active citizens in a deeply troubled and ethnically polarized nation and world.

The claim that multicultural education is only for ethnic groups of color and the disenfranchised is one of the most pernicious and damaging misconceptions with which the movement has to cope (Glazer, 1997). It has caused serious problems and has haunted the multicultural education movement since its inception. Despite everything written and spoken about multicultural education being for all students, the image of multicultural education as an entitlement program for the "others" remains strong and vivid in the public imagination as well as in the hearts and minds of many teachers and administrators. Teachers who teach in predominantly White schools and districts often state that they don't have a program or plan for multicultural education because they have few African American, Latino, or Asian American students.

When multicultural education is viewed by educators as the study of "the other," it is marginalized and prevented from becoming a part of mainstream educational reform. Several critics of multicultural education, such as Schlesinger (1991), Glazer (1997), and Gray (1991), have perpetuated the idea that multicultural education is the study of the "other" by defining it as the same as Afrocentric education.

The history of intergroup education teaches us that only when educational reform related to diversity is viewed as essential for all students—and as promoting the broad public interest—will it have a reasonable chance of becoming institutionalized in the nation's schools, colleges, and universities (C. A. M. Banks, 1996b). The intergroup education movement of the 1940s and 1950s failed in large part because intergroup educators were never able to get mainstream educators to believe that it was needed by and designed for all students (Taba, Brady, & Robinson, 1952). To its bitter and quiet end, intergroup education was viewed as something for schools with racial problems and as something for "them" and not for "us."

Multicultural Education Is Against the West

Another harmful misconception of multicultural education has been repeated so often by its critics that it is frequently viewed by readers as self-evident. This is the claim that multicultural education is a movement against the West and Western civilization. Multicultural education is not against the West because most writers of color—such as Rudolfo A. Anaya, Paula Gunn Allen, N. Scott Momaday, Maxine Hong Kingston, Maya Angelou, and Toni Morrison—are Western. Multicultural education itself is a thoroughly Western movement. It grew out of a civil rights movement grounded in Western democratic ideals such as freedom, justice, and equality. Multicultural education seeks to expand for all people ideals that were meant for an elite few at the nation's beginning (Foner, 1998; Franklin, 1989).

Although multicultural education is not against the West, its theorists do advocate that the truth about the West should be told, that its debt to people of color and women be recognized and included in the curriculum, and that the discrepancies between the ideals of freedom and equality, and the realities of racism and sexism, be taught to students. Reflective citizen action is also an integral part of multicultural theory. Multicultural education views citizen action to improve society as an integral part of education in a democracy. It links knowledge, values, empowerment, and action (Banks, 1996c). Multicultural education is postmodern in its assumptions about knowledge and knowledge construction. It challenges Enlightenment, positivist assumptions about the relationship between human values, knowledge, and action.

Positivists, who are heirs of the Enlightenment, believe that it is possible to structure knowledge that is objective and beyond human values and interests. Multicultural theorists maintain that knowledge is positional, that is relates to the knower's values and experiences, and that knowledge implies action (Harding, 1998). Consequently, different concepts, theories, and paradigms imply different kinds of actions. Multiculturalists believe that in order to have valid knowledge, information about the social condition and experiences of the knower is essential (Code, 1991; Collins, 2000).

A few critics of multicultural education, such as Leo (2000) and D'Souza (1991), claim that multicultural education has reduced or displaced the study of Western civilization in the nation's schools, colleges, and universities. As Gerald Graff (1992) points out in his informative book, *Beyond the Cultural Wars,* this claim is simply not true. Graff cites research by himself at the college level and by Applebee (1993) at the high school level to substantiate his conclusion that European and American male authors such as Shakespeare, Dante, Chaucer, Twain, and Hemingway still dominate the required reading lists in the nation's high schools, colleges, and universities. Graff found that most of the books by authors of color in the cases he examined were optional rather than required readings. Applebee found that of the ten most frequently assigned, required book-length works taught in the high school grades, only one title was by a female author (Harper Lee, *To Kill a Mockingbird*), and none was by a writer of color. Works by Shakespeare, Steinbeck, and Dickens lead the list.

Multicultural Education Will Divide the Nation

Many of its critics claim that multicultural education will divide the nation and undercut its unity. Schlesinger (1991) underscores this view by titling his book, *The Disuniting of America: Reflections on a Multicultural Society.* This misconception of multicultural education is based partly on questionable assumptions about the nature of U.S. society and partly on a mistaken view about multicultural education. The claim that multicultural education will divide the nation assumes that the nation is already united. While we are one nation politically, sociologically our nation is deeply divided along race, gender, sexual orientation, and class lines. The results of the 2000 election indicated the deep divisions between African American and Whites. Over 90 percent of African Americans voted for Al Gore, while a majority of White men voted for George W. Bush.

Multicultural education is designed to help unify a deeply divided nation rather than to divide a highly cohesive one. Multicultural education supports the notion of *e pluribus unum*—out of many, one. The multiculturalists and the Western traditionalists, however, often differ about how the unum can best be attained. Traditionally, the larger U.S. society as well as the schools have tried to create the unum by assimilating students from diverse racial and ethnic groups into a mythical Anglo

American culture that required them to experience a process of self-alienation and harsh assimilation. However, even when students of color became culturally assimilated, they were often structurally excluded from mainstream institutions.

Multicultural educators view e pluribus unum as the appropriate national goal but believe that the goal must be negotiated, discussed, and restructured to reflect the nation's ethnic and cultural diversity. The reformulation of the unum must be a process and must involve the participation by diverse groups within the nation, such as people of color, women, straights, gays, the powerful, the powerless, the young, and the old. The reformulation of the unum must also involve power sharing and participation by people from many different cultural communities. They must discuss, debate, share power, experience equal status, and reach beyond their cultural and ethnic borders in order to create a common civic culture that reflects and contributes to the well-being of all. This common civic culture will extend beyond the cultural borders of each group and constitute a civic borderland culture.

In *Borderlands,* Gloria Anzaldua (1999) contrasts cultural borders and borderlands; she states the need to weaken cultural borders and to create a shared borderland culture in which people from many different cultures can interact, relate, and engage in civic talk and action. Anzaldua states that "borders are set up to define the places that are safe and unsafe, to distinguish us from them. A border is a dividing line, a narrow strip along a steep edge. A borderland is a vague and undetermined place created by the residue of an unnatural boundary. It is in a constant state of transition" (p. 3).

Progress in Multicultural Education

Multicultural Education Has Made Significant Curriculum Inroads

While it is still not the center of the curriculum in many schools and colleges, multicultural content has made significant inroads into both the school and the college curriculums within the last three decades. The truth lies somewhere between the claim that no progress has been made in infusing and transforming the school and college curriculum with ethnic content and the claim that such content has replaced the European and American classics.

In the elementary and high schools, much more ethnic content appears in social studies and language arts textbooks today than was the case thirty years ago. Also, some teachers assign works written by authors of color along with the more standard American classics. In his study of book-length works used in the high schools, Applebee (1993) concluded that his most striking findings were how similar present reading lists are to past ones and how little change has occurred. However, he noted that many teachers use anthologies as a mainstay of their literature programs and that 21 percent of the anthology selections were written by women and 14 percent by authors of color.

More classroom teachers today have studied multicultural education concepts than at any previous point in our nation's history. A significant percentage of today's classroom teachers took one of the required teacher education courses in multicultural education when they were in college. The multicultural education standard adopted by the National Council for the Accreditation of Teacher Education (1997) (NCATE) in 1977, which became effective January 1, 1979, was a major factor that stimulated the growth of multicultural education in teacher education programs. The standard, which was issued in revised form in 1997, includes a number of multicultural indicators, including this one: "Teaching reflects knowledge about and experiences with cultural diversity and exceptionalities" (p. 19).

The teacher education market in multicultural education textbooks is now a substantial one. Most major publishers currently publish several major college textbooks in the field. Most major textbooks in other required education courses, such as educational psychology and the foundations of education, have separate chapters or sections that examine concepts and developments in multicultural education.

Some of the nation's leading colleges and universities, such as the University of California, Berkeley, the University of Minnesota-Twin Cities, and Stanford University, have either revised their core to include ethnic content or have established an ethnic studies course requirement. However, the transformation of the traditional canon on college and university campuses has often been bitter and divisive. All curriculum changes come slowly and painfully to university campuses (Carnochan, 1993). The linkage of curriculum change with issues related to race evokes latent primordial feelings and reflects the racial crisis in U.S. society. On some campuses, such as the University of Washington, Seattle, a bitter struggle ended with the defeat of the ethnic studies requirement. Ironically, the undergraduate population of students of color at the University of Washington is increasing substantially. During the 1999–2000 academic year, they made up nearly one-third (30 percent) of the Washington undergraduate population, most of whom were Asian Americans (22.2 percent).

Changes are also coming to elementary and high school textbooks (J. Garcia, 1993). The demographic imperative is an important factor driving the changes in school textbooks. The color of the nation's students is changing rapidly. In 1995, 35 percent of the nation's public elementary and secondary students were students of color (Pratt & Rittenhouse, 1998). Table 1.1 shows the enrollment in public elementary and secondary schools by race or ethnicity in 1986 and in 1999–2000. It is projected that nearly half (about 45.5 percent) of the nation's school-age youth will be youth of color by the year 2020 (Pallas, Natriello, & McDill, 1989).

Language diversity is also increasing in the United States. In 1990, more than 17,000 Americans spoke Spanish at home (see Table 1.2). Parents of color and parents who speak a first language other than English are demanding that their leaders, images, pain, and dreams be mirrored in the textbooks that their children study in school.

Textbooks have always reflected the myths, hopes, and dreams of the people in society with money and power. As African Americans, Latinos, Asians, and women become more influential participants on the power stage, textbooks will increasingly reflect their hopes, dreams, and disappointments. Textbooks will have to survive in the marketplace of a browner America. Because textbooks still carry the curriculum in the nation's public schools, they will remain an important focus for multicultural curriculum reformers.

Multicultural Education and the Future

The attainments of multicultural education since the late sixties and early seventies are noteworthy and should be acknowledged. Its shapers have been able to establish goals, aims, and approaches on which there is a high level of agreement (Banks & Banks, 1995). Most multicultural education theorists agree that the major goal of multicultural education is to restructure schools so that all students will acquire the knowledge, atti-

TABLE 1.1 Enrollment in Public Elementary and Secondary Schools, by Race and Ethnicity, Fall 1986 and the 1999–2000 School Year

Group	Percent Distribution, Fall 1986	Percent Distribution, 1999–2000 School Year
White	70.4	62.1
Black	16.1	17.2
Hispanic	9.9	15.6
Asian or Pacific Islander	2.8	4.0
American Indian/Alaskan Native	.09	1.2

Source: National Center for Education Statistics (2001, January). *Statistics in Brief.* Washington, DC: U.S. Department of Education.

TABLE 1.2 Top Fifteen Languages Other Than English Spoken at Home: 1990 and 1980

Language	Number (thousands) 1990	Number (thousands) 1980	Percent Change, 1980–90
Spanish	17,345	11,116	56
French	1,930	*1,609	20
German	1,548	1,587	–2
Chinese	1,319	631	109
Italian	1,309	1,618	–19
Tagalog (Pilipino)	843	*452	87
Polish	723	821	–12
Korean	626	266	135
Vietnamese	507	195	161
Portuguese	431	352	22
Japanese	428	336	27
Greek	388	401	–3
Arabic	355	217	63
Hindi (Urdu)	331	*130	155
Russian	242	173	40

Source: U.S. Bureau of the Census (1994, February). *We asked...you told us: Languages spoken at home.* Washington, DC: U.S. Government Printing Office.

*Three years and over; all other figures, five years and over.

tudes, and skills needed to function in an ethnically and racially diverse nation and world. As in other interdisciplinary fields of study—such as the social studies, leadership, and special education—there are internal debates within the field. These debates are consistent with a field that values democracy and diversity. They are also a source of strength.

Multicultural education is experiencing impressive success in being implemented in the nation's schools, colleges, and universities. The number of national conferences, school district workshops, and teacher education courses in multicultural education are evidence of its success and perceived importance. It is increasingly becoming institutionalized in the nation's educational institutions. Although the process is slow and sometimes contentious, multicultural content is increasingly becoming a part of core courses in school, college, and university courses. Textbook publishers are also integrating their books with ethnic and cultural content (J. Garcia, 1993). The pace of the integration of ethnic content into textbooks is increasing.

Despite its impressive successes, multicultural education faces important challenges in the next few decades. The debate about diversity reflects the value dilemma and identity crisis in U.S. society. The American identity is being reshaped as groups on the margins of society begin to participate in the center and to demand that their visions be reflected in a transformed America. The power sharing and identity transformation required to make racial peace may be valued rather than feared in the future because of the contributions they will make to our national salvation.

As the ethnic texture of nations such as the United States, Canada, and the United Kingdom continues to deepen, educational programs related to ethnic and cultural diversity will continue to emerge and will take various shapes and forms. New challenges will continue to evolve in pluralistic democratic societies. The extent to which these challenges will be transformed into opportunities will be largely dependent on the vision, knowledge, and commitment of each nation's educators. You will have to take a stand on multicultural education and determine what actions related to it you will take in your classroom and school. The chapters in this book are designed to help you conceptualize and take informed and reflective actions that will make your school a more caring and humane place for all students.

CHAPTER

2 Dimensions and School Characteristics

Dimensions and School Characteristics

One problem that continues to haunt the multicultural education movement, from both within and without, is the tendency by the public, teachers, administrators, and policy makers to oversimplify the concept. Multicultural education is complex and multidimensional, yet media commentators and educators alike often focus on only one of its many dimensions. Some teachers view it only as the inclusion of content about ethnic groups into the curriculum; others view it as prejudice reduction; still others view it as the celebration of ethnic holidays and events. After a presentation in a school in which I described the major goals of multicultural education, a math teacher told me that what I said was fine and appropriate for language arts and social studies teachers but it had nothing to do with him. After all, he said, math was math, regardless of the color of the students.

The Dimensions of Multicultural Education

This statement by a respected teacher, and his reaction to multicultural education, caused me to think deeply about the images of multicultural education that had been created by the key theorists in the field. I wondered whether we were partly responsible for this teacher's narrow conception of multicultural education as merely content integration. It was in response to these kinds of statements by classroom teachers that I conceptualized the dimensions of multicultural education. I use the dimensions in this chapter to describe the field's major components and to highlight important developments within the last two decades (Banks, 1995b). The dimensions of multicultural education are (1) content integration, (2) the knowledge construction process, (3) prejudice reduction, (4) an equity pedagogy, and (5) an empowering school culture and social structure (see Figure 2.1)

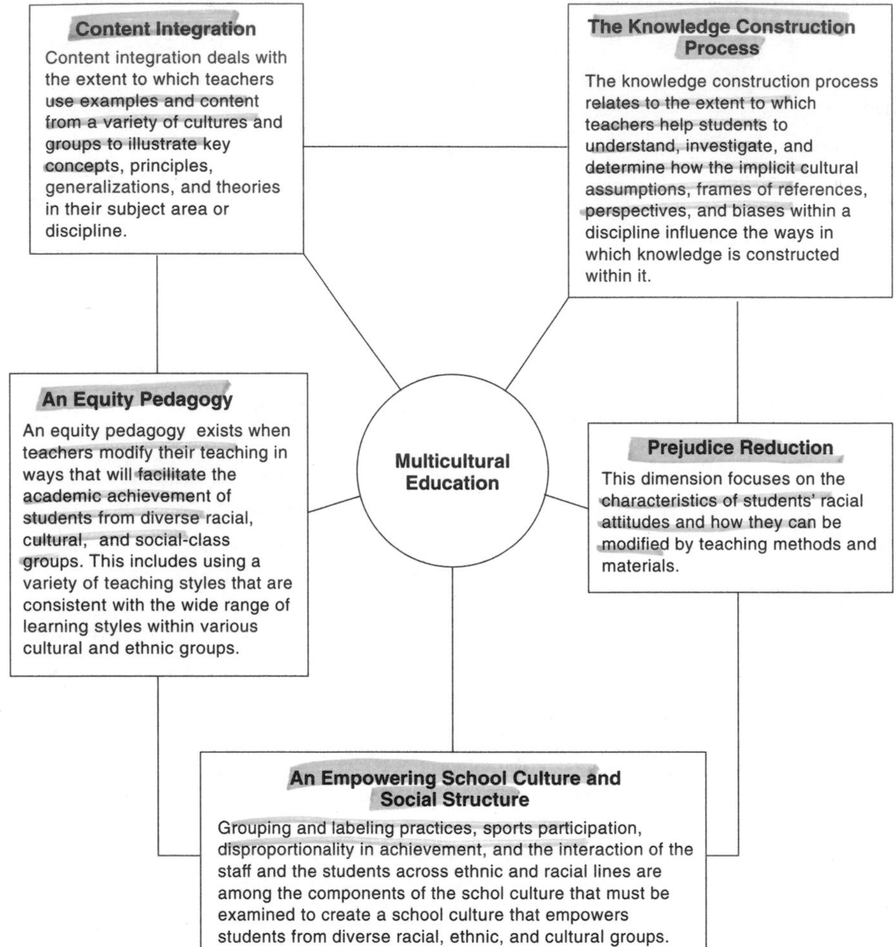

FIGURE 2.1 **The Dimensions of Multicultural Education**

Source: Reprinted with permission from James A. Banks (2001). *Cultural Diversity and Education: Foundations, Curriculum and Teaching* (4th ed.). Boston: Allyn and Bacon, p. 5.

Content Integration

Content integration deals with the extent to which teachers use examples, data, and information from a variety of cultures and groups to illustrate the key concepts, principles, generalizations, and theories in their subject area or discipline. In many school districts as well as in popular writings, multicultural education is viewed only—or primarily—as content integration. This narrow conception of multicultural education is a major reason that many teachers in subjects such as biology, physics, and mathematics believe that multicultural education is irrelevant to them and their students.

In fact, this dimension of multicultural education probably does have more relevance to social studies and language arts teachers than it does to physics and math teachers. Physics and math teachers can insert multicultural content into their subjects, for example, by using biographies of physicists and mathematicians of color and examples from different cultural groups. However, these kinds of activities are probably not the most important multicultural tasks that can be undertaken by science and math teachers. Activities related to the other dimensions of multicultural education, such as the knowledge construction process, prejudice reduction, and an equity pedagogy, are probably the most fruitful areas for the multicultural involvement of science and math teachers.

The Knowledge Construction Process

The knowledge construction process describes the procedures by which social, behavioral, and natural scientists create knowledge and how the implicit cultural assumptions, frames of references, perspectives, and biases within a discipline influence the ways that knowledge is constructed within it. The knowledge construction process is an important part of multicultural teaching. Teachers help students to understand how knowledge is created and how it is influenced by the racial, ethnic, gender, and social-class positions of individuals and groups.

Important and landmark work related to the construction of knowledge has been done within the last decade by feminist social scientists and epistemologists, as well as by scholars in ethnic studies. Working in philosophy and sociology, Sandra Harding (1991, 1998), Lorraine Code (1991), and Patricia Hill Collins (2000) have done some of the most important work in knowledge construction. This seminal work, although influential among scholars and curriculum developers, has been overshadowed in the popular media by the polarized canon debates. These writers and researchers have seriously challenged the claims made by the positivists that knowledge is value-free and have described the ways in which knowledge claims are influenced by the gender and ethnic characteristics of the knower. These scholars argue that the human interests and value assumptions of those who create knowledge should be identified, discussed, and examined.

Code (1991) states that the gender of the knower is epistemologically significant because knowledge is both *subjective* and *objective,* and that both aspects should be recognized and discussed. Collins (2000), an African American sociologist, extends and enriches the works of writers such as Code (1991) and Harding (1991) by describing the ways in which race and gender interact to influence knowledge construction. Collins calls the perspective of African American women, "the outsider-within perspective." She writes, "As outsiders within, Black women have a distinct view of the contradictions between the dominant group's actions and ideologies" (p. 11).

Curriculum theorists and developers in multicultural education are conceptualizing and developing ways to apply the work being done by the feminist and ethnic studies epistemologists to the classroom. In a book-length work, *Transforming Knowledge,* Elizabeth K. Minnich (1990), a professor of philosophy and women's studies, has analyzed the nature of knowledge and described how errors made within the dominant knowledge tradition contribute to the marginalization of women. These errors include faulty generalization, circular reasoning, mystified concepts, and partial knowledge.

Prejudice Reduction

The prejudice reduction dimension of multicultural education describes the characteristics of children's racial attitudes and strategies that can be used to help students to develop more positive racial and ethnic attitudes (Banks et al., 2001; Stephan, 1999). Since the 1960s, social scientists have learned a great deal about how racial attitudes in children develop and about ways in which educators can design interventions to help children to acquire more positive feelings toward other racial groups. I have reviewed that research in two other publications (Banks, 1995a; Banks, 1993c), and readers are referred to them for a comprehensive discussion of this topic. Aboud (1988) and Stephan (1999) also provide extensive discussions of the research on children's racial attitudes.

This research tells us that by the age of four African American, White, and Mexican American children are aware of racial differences and often make racial preferences that are biased toward Whites. Students can be helped to develop more positive racial attitudes if realistic images of ethnic and racial groups are included in teaching materials in a consistent, natural, and integrated fashion. Involving students in vicarious experiences and in cooperative learning activities with students of other racial groups will also help them to develop more positive racial attitudes and behaviors. Researchers such as Cross (1991) and Wright (1998) question the research that shows that African American children have negative attitudes toward themselves and other African Americans.

Equity Pedagogy

An equity pedagogy exists when teachers use techniques and teaching methods that facilitate the academic achievement of students from diverse racial, ethnic, and social-class groups. Using teaching techniques that cater to the learning and cultural styles of diverse groups (Shade, Kelly, & Oberg, 1997), and using cooperative learning techniques (Cohen & Lotan, 1997), are some of the teaching techniques that teachers have found effective with students from diverse racial, ethnic, and language groups.

If teachers are to increase learning opportunities for all students, they must be knowledgeable about the social and cultural contexts of teaching and learning (Banks et al., 2001). Although students are not solely products of their cultures and vary in the degree to which they identify with them, there are some distinctive cultural behaviors associated with ethnic groups (Au, 1979; Boykin, 1986). Effective teachers are aware of the distinctive backgrounds of their students and have the skills to translate that knowledge into effective instruction (Gay, 2000).

Research indicates that teachers can increase the classroom participation and academic achievement of students from different ethnic groups by modifying their instruction so that it draws upon their cultural strengths. In Susan Philips's study (1983) on the Warm Spring Indian Reservation in Oregon, American Indian students participated more actively in class discussions when teachers used group-oriented participation structures that were consistent with their community cultures. Researchers Kathryn Au (1979) and Roland G. Tharp (1982), working in the Kamehameha Early Education Program (KEEP), found that both student participation and standardized achievement test scores increased when they incorporated teaching strategies consistent with the cultures of Native Hawaiian students and used the children's experiences in reading instruction.

An Empowering School Culture and Social Structure

An empowering school culture and social structure describes the process of restructuring the culture and organization of the school so that students from diverse racial, ethnic, and social-class groups will experience educational equality and empowerment. This dimension of multicultural education involves conceptualizing the school as a unit of change and making structural changes within the school environment so that students from all social-class, racial, ethnic, and gender groups will have an equal opportunity for success. Establishing assessment techniques that are fair to all groups (Mercer, 1989, Armour-Thomas & Gopaul-McNicol, 1998), detracking the school (Wells, Hirshberg, Lipton, & Oaks, 1995), and creating the norm among the school staff that all students can learn, regardless of their racial, ethnic, or social-class groups, are important goals for schools that wish to create a school culture and social structure that is empowering and enhancing for students from diverse groups.

Characteristics of a Multicultural School

To implement the dimensions of multicultural education, schools and other educational institutions must be reformed so that students from all social-class, racial, cultural, and language groups and from both gender groups will have an equal opportunity to learn and experience cultural empowerment (Banks & Banks, 2001). Educational institutions should also help all students to develop more democratic values and beliefs and the knowledge, skills, and attitudes needed to function cross-culturally.

What parts of the school need to be reformed in order to implement the dimensions of multicultural education? A reformed school that exemplifies the dimensions has the eight characteristics listed in Table 2.1. Consequently, school reform should be targeted on the following school variables:

1. *Attitudes, perceptions, beliefs, and actions of the school staff.* Research indicates that teachers and administrators often have low expectations for language minority students (August & Hakuta, 1997; Heath, 1983), low-income students, and students of color (Philips, 1983). In a restructured multicultural school, teachers and administrators have high academic expectations for all students and believe that all students can learn (Brookover et al., 1979; Edmonds, 1986; Ladson-Billings, 1994).

2. *Formalized curriculum and course of study.* The curriculum in most schools shows most concepts, events, and situations from the perspectives of mainstream Americans (Applebee, 1993). It often marginalizes the experiences of people of color and of women. Multicultural education reforms the curriculum so that students view events, concepts, issues, and problems from the perspectives of diverse racial, ethnic, language, and social-class groups (Banks, 1997b). The perspectives of both men and women are also important in the restructured, multicultural curriculum.

3. *Learning, teaching, and cultural styles favored by the school.* Research indicates that a large number of low-income, linguistic minority, Latino, Native American, and African American students have learning, cultural, and motivational characteristics that differ from the teaching styles that are used most frequently in the schools (Delpit, 1995; Ramírez & Castañeda, 1974; Shade, Kelly, & Oberg, 1997). These students often learn best

TABLE 2.1 The Eight Characteristics of the Multicultural School

1. The teachers and school administrators have high expectations for all students and positive attitudes toward them. They also respond to them in positive and caring ways.
2. The formalized curriculum reflects the experiences, cultures, and perspectives of a range of cultural and ethnic groups as well as of both genders.
3. The teaching styles used by the teachers match the learning, cultural, and motivational styles of the students.
4. The teachers and administrators show respect for the students' first languages and dialects.
5. The instructional materials used in the school show events, situations, and concepts from the perspectives of a range of cultural, ethnic, and racial groups.
6. The assessment and testing procedures used in the school are culturally sensitive and result in students of color being represented proportionately in classes for the gifted and talented.
7. The school culture and the hidden curriculum reflect cultural and ethnic diversity.
8. The school counselors have high expectations for students from different racial, ethnic, and language groups and help these students to set and realize positive career goals.

when cooperative rather than competitive teaching techniques are used (Cohen & Lotan, 1997; Slavin, 1983; Stahl & VanSickle, 1992). Many of them also learn best when school rules and learning outcomes are made explicit and expectations are made clear (Delpit, 1997).

4. *Languages and dialects of the school*. Many students come to school speaking languages and dialects of English that differ from the standard English being taught. Although all students must learn standard English in order to function successfully in the wider society, the school should respect the first languages and varieties of English that students speak. Many African American students come to school speaking what many linguists call Ebonics or "Black English" (Perry & Delpit, 1998; Smitherman, 2000). In the restructured, multicultural school, teachers and administrators respect the languages and dialects of English that students come to school speaking and use the students' first languages and dialects as vehicles for helping them to learn standard English (Heath, 1983; Ovando & Collier, 1998).

5. *Instructional materials*. Many biases—sometimes latent—are found in textbooks and other instructional materials (Apple & Christian-Smith, 1991). These materials often marginalize the experiences of people of

color, women, and low-income people and focus on the perspectives of men who are members of the mainstream society. In the restructured, multicultural school, instructional materials are reformed and depict events from diverse ethnic and cultural perspectives. Teachers and students are also taught to identify and challenge the biases and assumptions of all materials.

6. *Assessment and testing procedures.* IQ and other mental-ability tests often result in students of color, low-income students, and linguistic minority students being overrepresented in classes for students with mental retardation and underrepresented in classes for students who are gifted and talented (Armour-Thomas & Gopaul-McNicol, 1998; Ford, 1996). Human talent, as well as mental retardation, is randomly distributed across human population groups (Gardner, 1983). Consequently, in a restructured multicultural school, assessment techniques are used that enable students from diverse cultural, ethnic, and language groups to be assessed in culturally fair and just ways (Armour-Thomas & Gopaul-McNicol, 1998; Mercer, 1989). In a restructured multicultural school, students of color and language minority students are found proportionately in classes for the gifted and talented (Ford, 1996). They are not heavily concentrated in classes for mentally retarded students (Artiles & Zamora-Durán, 1997).

7. *The school culture and the hidden curriculum.* The hidden curriculum has been defined as the curriculum that no teacher explicitly teaches but that all students learn. The school's attitudes toward cultural and ethnic diversity are reflected in many subtle ways in the school culture, such as the kinds of pictures on the bulletin boards, the racial composition of the school staff, and the fairness with which students from different racial, cultural, and ethnic groups are disciplined and suspended. Multicultural education reforms the total school environment so that the hidden curriculum sends the message that cultural and ethnic diversity is valued and celebrated.

8. *The counseling program.* In an effective multicultural school, counselors help students from diverse cultural, racial, and ethnic groups to make effective career choices and to take the courses needed to pursue those career choices (Ponterotto, Casas, Suzuki, & Alexander, 1995; Sue, 1995). Multiculturally oriented counselors also help students to reach beyond their grasp, to dream, and to actualize their dreams.

Multicultural educators make the assumption that if the preceding eight variables within the school environment are reformed and restructured and the dimensions of multicultural education are implemented, students from diverse ethnic, cultural, and language groups and of both genders will attain higher levels of academic achievement and the intergroup attitudes and beliefs of students from all groups will become more democratic.

CHAPTER

3 Curriculum Transformation

It is important to distinguish between curriculum *infusion* and curriculum *transformation.* When the curriculum is infused with ethnic and gender content without curriculum transformation, the students view the experiences of ethnic groups and of women from the perspectives and conceptual frameworks of the traditional Western canon. Consequently, groups such as Native Americans, Asian Americans, and Latinos are added to the curriculum, but their experiences are viewed from the perspective of mainstream historians and social scientists. When curriculum infusion occurs without transformation, women are added to the curriculum but are viewed from the perspectives of mainstream males. Concepts such as "The Westward Movement," "The European Discovery of America," and "Men and Their Families Went West" remain intact.

When curriculum transformation occurs, students and teachers make paradigm shifts and view the American and world experience from the perspectives of different racial, ethnic, cultural, and gender groups. Columbus's arrival in the Americas is no longer viewed as a "discovery" but as a cultural contact or encounter that had very different consequences for the Tainos (Arawaks), Europeans, and Africans (Golden et al., 1991; Rouse, 1992; Stannard, 1992). In a transformed curriculum, the experiences of women in the West are not viewed as an appendage to the experience of men but "through women's eyes" (Armitage, 1987; Limerick, 1987).

This chapter discusses the confusion over goals in multicultural education, describes its goals and challenges, and states the rationale for a transformative multicultural curriculum. Important goals of multicultural education are to help teachers and students transform their thinking about the nature and development of the United States and the world and also to develop a commitment to act in ways that will make the United States a more democratic and just nation.

Confusion Over the Meaning of Multicultural Education

A great deal of confusion exists, among both educators and the general public, about the meaning of multicultural education. The meaning of multicultural education among these groups varies from education about people in other lands to educating African American students about their heritage but teaching them little about the Western heritage of the United States. The confusion over the meaning of multicultural education was indicated by a question the editor of a national education publication asked me: "What is the difference between multicultural education, ethnocentric education, and global education?" Later during the telephone interview, I realized that she had meant "Afrocentric education" rather than "ethnocentric education." To her, these terms were synonymous.

The Meaning and Goals of Multicultural Education

Before we can solve the problem caused by the multiple meanings of multicultural education, we need to better understand the causes of the problem. One important cause of the confusion over the meaning of multicultural education is the multiple meanings of the concept in the professional literature itself. Sleeter and Grant (1987), in their comprehensive survey of the literature on multicultural education, found that the term has diverse meanings and that about the only commonality the various definitions share is reform designed to improve schooling for students of color.

To advance the field and to reduce the multiple meanings of multicultural education, scholars need to develop a higher level of consensus about what the concept means. Agreement about the meaning of multicultural education is emerging among academics. A consensus is developing among scholars that an important goal of multicultural education is to increase educational equality for both gender groups, for students from diverse ethnic and cultural groups, and for exceptional students (Banks & Banks, 2001; Grant & Ladson-Billings, 1997; Grant & Tate, 1995). A major assumption of multicultural education is that some groups of students—because their cultural characteristics are more consistent with the culture, norms, and expectations of the school than are those of other groups of students—have greater opportunities for academic success than do students whose cultures are less consistent with the school culture. Low-income African American males, for example, tend to have more problems in schools than do middle-class White males (Gibbs, 1988).

Because one of its goals is to increase educational equality for students from diverse groups, school restructuring is essential to make multicultural education become a reality. To restructure schools in order to provide all students with an equal chance to learn, some of the major assumptions, beliefs, and structures within schools must be radically changed. These include tracking and the ways in which mental ability tests are interpreted and used (Armour-Thomas & Gopaul-McNicol, 1998; Mercer, 1989; Oakes, 1992). New paradigms about the ways students learn, about human ability (Gardner, 1983; Gould, 1981), and about the nature of knowledge will have to be institutionalized in order to restructure schools and make multicultural education a reality. Teachers will have to believe that all students can learn, regardless of their social-class or ethnic-group membership, and that knowledge is a social construction that has social, political, and normative assumptions (Banks, 2001; Code, 1991; Collins, 2000; Harding, 1991). Implementing multicultural education within a school is a continuous process that cannot be implemented within a few weeks or over several years. The implementation of multicultural education requires a long-term commitment to school improvement and restructuring.

Another important goal of multicultural education—on which there is wide consensus among authorities in the field but that is neither understood nor appreciated by many teachers, journalists, and the public—is to help all students, including White mainstream students, to develop the knowledge, skills, and attitudes they will need to survive and function effectively in a future U.S. society in which one out of every three people will be a person of color. Our survival as a strong and democratic nation will be seriously imperiled if we do not help our students attain the knowledge and skills they need to function in a culturally diverse future society and world. As Martin Luther King stated eloquently, "We will live together as brothers and sisters or die separate and apart as strangers" (King, 1987).

This goal of multicultural education is related to an important goal of global education—to help students to develop cross-cultural competency in cultures beyond our national boundaries and the insights and understandings needed to understand how all peoples living on the earth have highly interconnected fates (Diaz, Massialas, & Xanthopoulos, 1999). Citizens who have an understanding of and empathy for the cultures within their own nation are probably more likely to function effectively in cultures outside of their nation than are citizens who have little understanding of and empathy for cultures within their own society.

Although multicultural and global education share some important aims, in practice, global education can hinder teaching about ethnic and cultural diversity in the United States. Some teachers are more comfortable teaching about Mexico than they are teaching about Mexican Americans who live within their own cities and states. Other teachers, as well as some publishers, do not distinguish between multicultural and global education. Although the goals of multicultural and global education are complementary, they need to be distinguished both conceptually and in practice.

Multicultural Education Is for All Students

We need to think seriously about why multicultural educators have not been more successful in conveying to teachers, journalists, and the general public the idea that multicultural education is concerned not only with students of color and linguistically diverse students but also with White mainstream students. It is also not widely acknowledged that many of the reforms designed to increase the academic achievement of ethnic and linguistic minority students, such as a pedagogy that is sensitive to student learning styles and cooperative learning techniques, will also help White mainstream students to increase their academic achievement and to develop more positive intergroup attitudes and values (Cohen & Lotan, 1997; Gay, 2000; Shade, Kelly, & Oberg, 1997; Slavin, 1995).

It is important for multicultural education to be conceptualized as a strategy for all students for several important reasons. U.S. schools are not working as well as they should be to prepare all students to function in a highly technological, postindustrial society (Bell, 1973; Graham, 1992). Most students of color (with the important exception of some groups of Asian students such as Chinese Americans and Japanese Americans) and low-income students are more dependent on the school for academic achievement than are White middle-class students for a variety of complex reasons. However, school restructuring is needed for all students because of the high level of literacy and skills needed by citizens in a knowledge society and because of the high expectations that the public has for today's schools. Public expectations for the public schools have increased tremendously since the turn of the century, when many school leavers were able to get jobs in factories (Cremin, 1989; Graham, 1992). School restructuring is an important and major aim of multicultural education.

Multicultural education should also be conceptualized as a strategy for all students because it will become institutionalized and supported in the nation's schools, colleges, and universities only to the extent that it is perceived as universal and in the broad public interest. An ethnic-specific notion of multicultural education stands little chance of success and implementation in the nation's educational institutions.

Challenges to the Mainstream Curriculum

Some readers might rightly claim that an ethnic-specific curriculum and education already exists in the nation's educational institutions and that it is Eurocentric and male dominated. I would agree to some extent with this claim. However, I believe that the days for the primacy and dominance of the mainstream curriculum are limited. The curriculum that is institutionalized within our nation's schools, colleges, and universities is being seriously challenged today and will continue to be challenged until it is reformed and more accurately reflects the experiences, voices, and struggles of people of color, of women, and of other cultural, language, and social-class groups in U.S. society. The curriculum within our nation's schools, colleges, and universities has changed substantially within the last three decades. It is important that these changes be recognized and acknowledged. Students in today's educational institutions are learning much more content about ethnic, cultural, racial, and gender diversity than they learned three decades ago. The ethnic studies and women's studies movements have had a significant influence on the curriculum in the nation's schools, colleges, and universities.

The dominance of the mainstream curriculum is much less complete and tenacious than it was before the Civil Rights and Women's Rights Movements of the 1960s and 1970s. The historical, social, and economic factors are different today than they were when Anglo Americans established control over the nation's major social, economic, and political institutions in the seventeenth and eighteenth centuries. The economic, demographic, and ideological factors that led to the establishment of Anglo hegemony early in our nation's history are changing, even though Anglo Americans are still politically, economically, and culturally dominant. Anglo dominance was indicated by the Supreme Court decisions that slowed the pace of affirmative action during the 1980s and that chipped away at civil rights laws protecting people with disabilities in 2001.

Nevertheless, there are signs throughout U.S. society that Anglo dominance and hegemony are being challenged and that groups such as African Americans, Asian Americans, and Latinos are increasingly demanding full structural inclusion and a reformulation of the canon used to select content for the school, college, and university curriculum (Butler & Walter, 1991; Graff, 1992). It is also important to realize that many compassionate and informed Whites are joining people of color to support reforms in the nation's social, economic, political, and educational institutions. It would be a mistake to conceptualize or perceive the reform movements today as people of color versus Whites.

One pervasive myth within our society is that Whites are a monolithic group. The word *White* conceals more than it reveals. Whites are a very diverse group in terms of ethnic and cultural characteristics, political affiliations, and attitudes toward ethnic and cultural diversity (Fine, Weis, Powell, & Wong, 1997; Howard, 1999). Many Whites today, as well as historically, have supported social movements to increase the rights of

African Americans and other people of color (Branch, 1988). Reform-oriented White citizens who are pushing for a more equitable and just society are an important factor that will make it increasingly difficult for the Anglo mainstream vision to continue to dominate U.S. political and educational institutions.

Whites today are playing an important role in social reform movements and in the election of African American and Latino politicians. Many White students on university campuses are forming coalitions with students of color to demand that the university curriculum be reformed to include content about people of color and women. The student movements that are demanding ethnic studies requirements on university campuses have experienced major victories (Hu-DeHart, 1995).

The Anglo-centric curriculum will continue to be challenged until it is reformed to include the voices and experiences of a range of ethnic, cultural, and language groups. The significant percentage of people of color, including African Americans and Latinos, who are in positions of leadership in educational institutions will continue to work to get the experiences of their people integrated into the school and university curriculum. These individuals include researchers, professors, administrators, and authors of textbooks. Students of color will continue to form coalitions with progressive White students and demand that the school and university curriculum be reformed to reflect the ethnic and cultural reality of U.S. society. Demographers project that students of color will make up about 46 percent of the nation's school-age youths (ages 0 to 17) by 2020 (Pallas, Natriello, & McDill, 1989). Parents and community groups will continue to demand that the school and university curriculum be reformed to give voice to their experiences and struggles. African American parents and community groups will continue to push for a curriculum that reflects African civilizations and experimental schools for Black males (Chmelynski, 1990; Lee, 1993).

Feminists will continue to challenge the mainstream curriculum because many of them view it as male-centric, patriarchal, and sexist. Much of the new research in women's studies deals with the cultures of women of color (Anderson & Collins, 1992; Hine, King, & Reed, 1995; Jones, 1985). Women's studies and ethnic studies will continue to interconnect and challenge the dominant curriculum in the nation's schools, colleges, and universities.

Challenges to Multicultural Education

I have argued that an ethnic-specific version of multicultural education is not likely to become institutionalized within the nation's schools, colleges, and universities and that the days of Anglo hegemony in the U.S. curriculum are limited. This is admittedly a long view of our society and future. Multicultural education is frequently challenged by conservative writers and groups (D'Souza, 1995; Leo, 2000; Schlesinger, 1991). This challenge is likely to continue, and will take diverse forms, expressions, and shapes. I believe that part of the confused meanings of multicultural education results from the attempts by neoconservative scholars to portray multicultural education as a movement against Western civilization, as anti-White, and by implication, as anti-American (Leo, 2000; Ravitch, 1990a; Sirkin, 1990). The popular press frequently calls the movement to infuse an African perspective into the curriculum "Afrocentric," and it has defined the term to mean an education that excludes Whites and Western civilization (Daley, 1990).

The term *Afrocentric* has different meanings to different people. Because of its diverse interpretations by various people and groups, neoconservative scholars have focused many of their criticisms of multicultural education on this concept. Asante (1998) defines Afrocentricity as "placing African ideals at the center of any analysis that involves African culture and behavior" (p. 6). In other words, he defines Afrocentricity as looking at African and African American behavior from an African or African American perspective. His definition suggests that Black English, or Ebonics, cannot be understood unless it is viewed from the perspective of those who speak it. Afrocentricity, when Asante's definition is used, can describe the addition of an African American perspective to the school and university curriculum. When understood in this way, it is consistent with a multicultural curriculum because a multicultural curriculum helps students to view behavior, concepts, and issues from different ethnic and cultural perspectives.

The Canon Battle: Special Interests versus the Public Interest

The push by people of color and women to get their voices and experiences institutionalized within the curriculum and the curriculum canon transformed has evoked a strong reaction from neoconservative scholars. Consequently, a battle over the canon between people of color, feminist scholars, and neoconservative scholars is taking place. The neoconservatives have founded two organizations to resist multicultural education: the Madison Center and the National Association of Scholars. The resistance to multicultural education has been strongly expressed in a series of editorials and articles in popular and educational publications (Finn, 1990; McConnell & Breindel, 1990; Ravitch, 1990a, 1990b; Leo, 2000), as well as in several best-selling books (D'Souza, 1991; Schlesinger, 1991).

Many of the arguments in the editorials and articles written by the opponents of multicultural education are smoke screens for a conservative political agenda designed not to promote the common good of the nation but to reinforce the status quo and dominant group hegemony and to promote the interests of a small elite. A clever tactic of the neoconservative scholars is to define their own interests as universal and in the public good and the interests of women and people of color as special interests that are particularistic (Ravitch, 1990a). When a dominant elite describes its interests as the same as the public interests, it marginalizes the experiences of structurally excluded groups, such as women and people of color.

The term *special interest* implies an interest that is particularistic and inconsistent with the overarching goals and needs of the nation-state or commonwealth. To be in the public good, interests must extend beyond the needs of a unique or particular group. An important issue is who formulates the criteria for determining what is a special interest. It is the dominant group or groups in power that have already shaped the curriculum, institutions, and structures in their images and interests. The dominant group views its interests not as special but as identical with the common good. A special interest, in the view of those who control the curriculum and other institutions within society, is therefore any interest that challenges their power and dominant ideologies and paradigms, particularly if the interest group demands that the canon, assumptions, and values of the institutions and structures be transformed. History is replete with examples of dominant groups that defined their interests as the public interest.

One way in which people in power marginalize and disempower those who are structurally excluded from the mainstream is by calling their visions, histories, goals, and struggles special interests. This type of marginalization denies the legitimacy and validity of groups that are excluded from full participation in society and its institutions.

Only a curriculum that reflects the experiences of a wide range of groups in the United States and the world, and the interests of these groups, is in the national interest and is consistent with the public good. Any other kind of curriculum reflects a special interest and is inconsistent with the needs of a nation that must survive in a pluralistic and highly interdependent world. Special interest history and literature, such as history and literature that emphasize the primacy of the West and the history of European American males, is detrimental to the public good because it will not help students to acquire the knowledge, skills, and attitudes essential for survival in the twenty-first century.

The aim of the ethnic studies and women's studies movements are not to push for special interests but to reform the curriculum so that it will be more truthful and more inclusive and will reflect the histories and experiences of the diverse groups and cultures that make up U.S. society. Rather than being special interest reform movements, they contribute to the democratization of the school and university curriculum. They contribute to the public good rather than to the strengthening of special interests.

We need to rethink concepts such as special interests, the national interest, and the public good and to identify which groups are using these terms and for what purposes, and also to evaluate the use of these terms in the context of a nation and world that is rapidly changing. Powerless and excluded groups accurately perceive efforts to label their visions and experiences *special interests* as an attempt to marginalize them and to make their voices silent and their faces invisible.

School Knowledge and Multicultural Literacy

Our concept of cultural literacy should be broader than the one presented by Hirsch (1987) in his book, *Cultural Literacy: What Every American Needs to Know.* Hirsch writes as if knowledge is neutral and static. His book contains a list of important facts that he believes students should master in order to become culturally literate. *Knowledge is dynamic, changing, and constructed within a social context rather than neutral and static,* as Hirsch implies. Hirsch recommends transmitting knowledge in a largely uncritical way. When we help students to attain knowledge, we should help them to recognize that knowledge reflects the social context in which it is created and that it has normative and value assumptions (Banks, 1996c).

I agree with Hirsch that there is a need for all U.S. citizens to have a common core of knowledge. However, the important questions are: Who will participate in the formulations of that knowledge? and Whose interests will it serve? We need a broad level of participation in the identification, construction, and formulation of the knowledge that we expect all of our citizens to master. Such knowledge should reflect cultural democracy and serve the needs of the diverse groups that make up the nation's population. It should contribute to public virtue and the public good. Such knowledge should not serve the needs of dominant and powerful groups, as much school and university knowledge does today. Rather, school knowledge should reflect the experiences of all of the nation's citizens, and it should empower all people to participate effectively in a democratic society. It should help to empower all citizens and encourage them to participate in civic discourse and citizen action..

A Transformed Curriculum and Multiple Perspectives

Educators use several approaches, summarized in Figure 3.1, to integrate cultural content into the school and university curriculum (Banks,1988a,

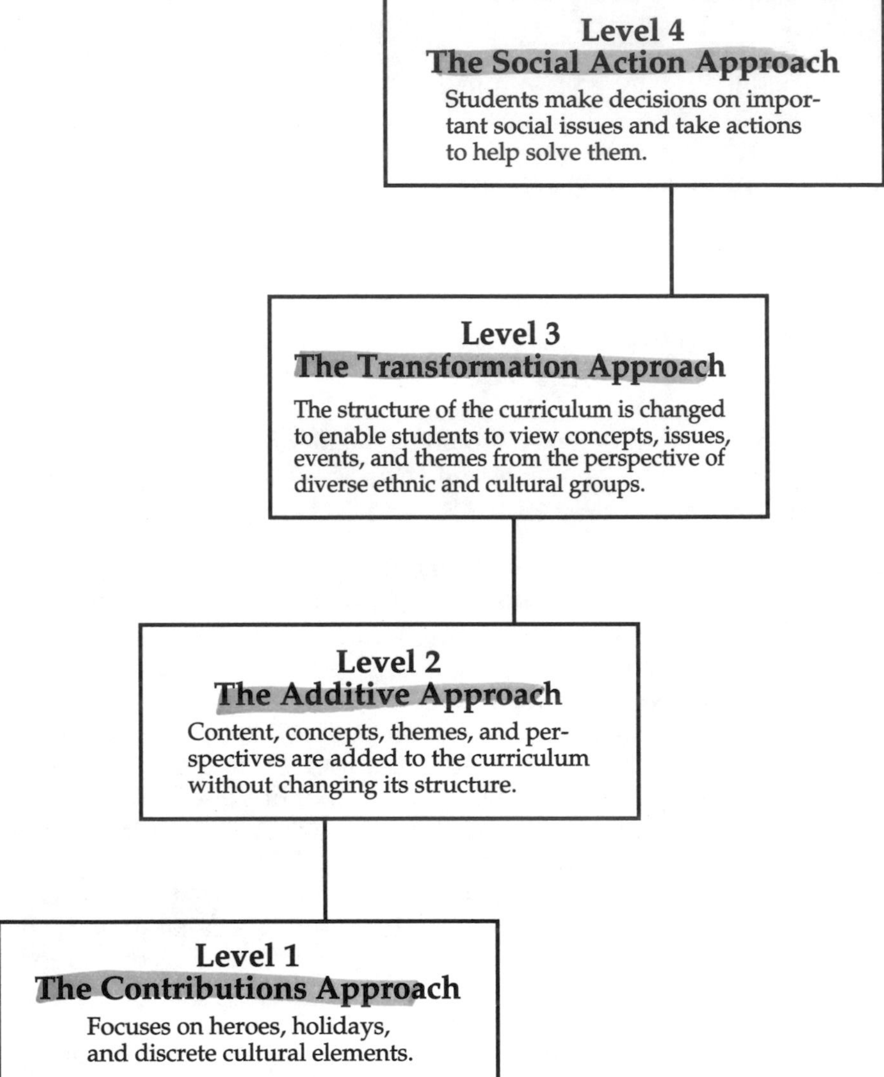

FIGURE 3.1 Approaches to Multicultural Curriculum Reform

1997b). These approaches include the *contributions approach,* in which content about ethnic and cultural groups are limited primarily to holidays and celebrations, such as Cinco de Mayo, Asian/Pacific Heritage Week, African American History Month, and Women's History Week. This approach is used often in the primary and elementary grades. Another frequently used approach to integrate cultural content into the curriculum is the *additive approach.* In this approach, cultural content, concepts, and themes are added to the curriculum without changing its basic structure, purposes, and characteristics. The additive approach is often accomplished by the addition of a book, a unit, or a course to the curriculum without changing its framework

Neither the contributions nor the additive approach challenges the basic structure or canon of the curriculum. Cultural celebrations, activities, and content are inserted into the curriculum within the existing curriculum framework and assumptions. When these approaches are used to integrate cultural content into the curriculum, people, events, and interpretations related to ethnic groups and women often reflect the norms and values of the dominant culture rather than those of cultural communities. Consequently, most of the ethnic groups and women added to the curriculum have values and roles consistent with those of the dominant culture. Men and women who challenged the status quo and dominant institutions are less likely to be selected for inclusion into the curriculum. Thus, Sacajawea is more likely to be chosen for inclusion than is Geronimo because she helped Whites to conquer Native American lands. Geronimo resisted the takeover of Native American lands by Whites.

The *transformation approach* differs fundamentally from the contributions and additive approaches. It changes the canon, paradigms, and basic assumptions of the curriculum and enables students to view concepts, issues, themes, and problems from different perspectives and points of view. Major goals of this approach include helping students to understand concepts, events, and people from diverse ethnic and cultural perspectives and to understand knowledge as a social construction. In this approach, students are able to read and listen to the voices of the victors and the vanquished. They are also helped to analyze the teacher's perspective on events and situations and are given the opportunity to formulate and justify their own versions of events and situations. Important aims of the transformation approach are to teach students to think critically and to develop the skills to formulate, document, and justify their conclusions and generalizations.

When teaching a unit such as "The Westward Movement" using a transformation approach, the teacher would assign appropriate readings and then ask the students such questions as: What do you think "The Westward Movement" means? Who was moving West—the Whites or the Native Americans? What region in the United States was referred to as the West? Why? The aim of these questions is to help students to understand that the *Westward Movement* is a Eurocentric term because the Lakota Sioux were already living in the West and consequently were not moving. As Patricia N. Limerick (2000) insightfully points out, the Native Americans were trying hard to stay put. They did not want to move.

"Westward Movement" is used to refer to the movement of the European Americans who were headed in the direction of the Pacific Ocean. The Sioux did not consider their homeland "the West" but the center of the universe. The teacher could also ask the students to describe the Westward Movement from the point of view of the Sioux. The students might use such words as "The End," "The Age of Doom," or "The Coming of the People Who Took Our Land." The teacher could also ask the students to give the unit a name that is more neutral than "The Westward Movement." They might name the unit "The Meeting of Two Cultures."

The *decision-making and social action approach* extends the transformative curriculum by enabling students to pursue projects and activities that allow them to take personal, social, and civic actions related to the concepts, problems, and issues they have studied. After they have studied the unit on different perspectives on The Westward Movement, the students might decide that they want to learn more about Native Americans and to take actions that will enable the school to depict and perpetuate more accurate and positive views of America's first inhabitants. The students might compile a list of books written by Native Americans for the school librarian to order and present a pageant for the school's morning exercise on "The Westward Movement: A View from the Other Side."

Teaching Students to Know, to Care, and to Act

Major goals of a transformative curriculum that fosters multicultural literacy should be to help students to know, to care, and to act in ways that will develop and foster a democratic and just society in which all groups experience cultural democracy and cultural empowerment. Knowledge is an essential part of multicultural literacy, but it is not sufficient. Knowledge alone will not help students to develop an empathetic, caring commitment to humane and democratic change. An essential goal of a multicultural curriculum is to help students to develop empathy and caring. To help our nation and world become more culturally democratic, students must also develop a commitment to personal, social, and civic action, as well as the knowledge and skills needed to participate in effective civic action.

Although knowledge, caring, and action are conceptually distinct, in the classroom they are highly interrelated. In my multicultural classes for teacher education students, I use historical and sociological knowledge about the experiences of different ethnic and racial groups to inform as well as to enable the students to examine and clarify their personal attitudes about ethnic diversity (see Chapter 7). These knowledge experiences are also a vehicle that enables the students to think of actions they can take to actualize their feelings and moral commitments.

Knowledge experiences that I have used to help students to examine their value commitments and to think of ways to act include the reading of *Balm in Gilead: Journey of a Healer,* Sara Lawrence Lightfoot's (1988) powerful biography of her mother, one of the nation's first African American child psychiatrists; the historical overviews of various U.S. ethnic groups in my book, *Teaching Strategies for Ethnic Studies* (Banks, 1997b); and several video and film presentations, including selected segments from *Eyes on the Prize II,* the award-winning history of the Civil Rights Movement produced by Henry Hampton, and *Eye of the Beholder,* a powerful videotape that uses simulation to show the cogent effects of discrimination on adults. The videotape features Jane Elliott, who attained fame for her well-known experiment in which she discriminated against children on the basis of eye color to teach them about discrimination (Peters, 1987).

To enable the students to analyze and clarify their values regarding these readings and video experiences, I ask them questions such as: How did the book, film, or videotape make you feel? Why do you think you feel that way? To enable them to think about ways to act on their feelings, I ask such questions as: How interracial are your own personal experiences? Would you like to live a more interracial life? What are some books that you can read or popular films that you can see that will enable you to act on your commitment to live a more racially and ethnically integrated life? The power of these kinds of experiences is often revealed in student papers, as is illustrated by this excerpt from a paper written by a student after he had viewed several segments of *Eyes on the Prize II* (Muir, 1990):

> I feel that my teaching will now necessarily be a little bit different forever simply because I myself have changed.... I am no longer quite the same person I was before I viewed the presentations—my horizons are a little wider, perspectives a little broader, insights a little deeper. That is what I gained from *Eyes on the Prize.*

The most meaningful and effective way to prepare teachers to involve students in multicultural experiences that will enable students to know, to care, and to participate in democratic action is to involve teachers in multicultural experiences that focus on these goals (see Chapter 7 for a further discussion of how I teach teacher education students about diversity and knowledge construction). When teachers have gained knowledge about cultural and ethnic diversity themselves, looked at that knowledge from different ethnic and cultural perspectives, and taken action to make their own lives and communities more culturally sensitive and diverse, they will have the knowledge and skills needed to help transform the curriculum canon as well the hearts and minds of their students. Only when the curriculum canon is transformed to reflect cultural diversity will students in our schools and colleges be able to attain the knowledge, skills, and perspectives needed to participate effectively in today's global society.

Multicultural Education and National Survival

Multicultural education is needed to help all of the nation's future citizens to acquire the knowledge, attitudes, and skills needed to survive in the twenty-first century. Nothing less than the nation's survival is at stake. The rapid growth in the nation's population of people of color, the escalating importance of non-White nations such as China and Japan, and the widening gap between the rich and the poor make it essential for our future citizens to have multicultural literacy and cross-cultural skills. A nation whose citizens cannot negotiate on the world's multicultural global stage will be tremendously disadvantaged in the twenty-first century, and its very survival may be imperiled.

CHAPTER

4 School Reform and Intergroup Education

Teachers and administrators for schools of today and tomorrow should acquire the knowledge, attitudes, and skills needed to work with students from diverse cultural groups and to help all students develop more positive racial attitudes. Teachers and administrators also need to restructure schools so that they will be able to deal effectively with the nation's growing diversity and to prepare future citizens who will be able to compete in a global world economy that will be knowledge and service oriented.

The first part of this chapter describes the demographic trends and developments related to the nation's changing ethnic texture and future workforce, states why school restructuring is essential in order to prepare the workforce needed for tomorrow, and describes the major variables of multicultural school reform.

The second part describes the characteristics of children's racial attitudes, and guidelines for helping students to acquire more positive racial attitudes, values, beliefs, and actions. This knowledge is essential for the preparation of teachers and administrators who will work in today's culturally, racially, and language-diverse schools.

Demographic Trends and the Changing Workforce

The U.S. workforce faces several major problems that have important implications for the professional work of teachers and administrators. Teachers and administrators need to be aware of these trends and to take part in school reform efforts designed to restructure our schools and institutions of higher education so that they will be able to respond to these demographic trends sensitively and reflectively. I call these trends the *demographic imperative.*

The United States will have a large number of people retiring and too few new workers entering the workforce during the next few decades. Our population is also becoming increasingly older. In 1980, about 12.5 percent of the nation's population consisted of people over age sixty-five. By 2030, 22 percent of the nation's population will be in that age group (Richman, 1990). The cost of supporting older workers will continue to mount in the coming decades. We will be dependent on fewer workers to provide social security funds for retirees. In the boom years of the 1950s, 17 workers supported every retiree. The ratio now is about three workers to one retiree. One of about every three of these workers is a person of color (U.S. Department of Labor, 2001). If the education of students of color does not improve significantly and quickly, a large number of the workers depended on to contribute to the incomes of retired workers will not have the skills and knowledge to participate effectively in a workforce that will be knowledge and service oriented.

The nation's economy is becoming increasingly global. Foreign investment in the United States grew from $90 billion in 1980 to $811,756 billion in 1998 (U.S. Census Bureau, 2000). The United States, as well as the other modernized nations, have moved from agricultural, to industrial, to knowledge/service societies. Bell (1973) calls these kinds of societies *post-industrial;* Toffler (1980) calls them *third wave.* Workers in this century must have the knowledge, attitudes, and skills needed to compete in a global world economy that is primarily service oriented. Most of the new wealth created today is in service industries (Johnson & Packer, 1987). Moreover, U.S. employers do not limit their search for skilled knowledge workers to the boundaries of this nation. U.S. workers have to compete with skilled knowledge workers throughout the world.

People of color will constitute an increasingly larger percentage of the workforce as we move further into this century. Whites made up 74 percent of the labor force in 1998. Their share of the labor force will decrease gradually and constitute 71 percent of the labor force by 2008 (U.S. Department of Labor, 2001). If these labor trends continue, there will be a mismatch between the knowledge and skill demands of the workforce and the knowledge and skills of a large proportion of U.S. workers. In 1998, about 26 percent of the labor force was made up of people of color. Their percentage of the workforce will gradually increase in the coming decades.

Workforce Needs in the Twenty-First Century

Knowledge-oriented service jobs, in fields such as education, health, and trade, require high-level reasoning and analytical, quantitative, and communication skills. Most corporations today have a transnational identity and find skilled workers to complete required jobs in any nation or part of the world.

In a segment of the PBS series *Learning in America,* it was revealed that a New York insurance company was sending paperwork by plane to Dublin, at regular intervals, to be done by workers there because the company regarded these workers as more competent than comparable workers in the United States. This U.S. insurance company was sending work to Dublin to be done at the same time that the unemployment rate among African American teenagers was as high as 30 to 40 percent in some inner-city communities.

The sending of work abroad foreshadows a trend that is likely to escalate in the future and pose serious problems for the development of productive U.S. citizens among ethnic groups of color in the United States. There is a growing need for highly skilled and technical workers in the United States and throughout the world. Yet, if the current levels of educational attainments among most U.S. youths of color continue, the nation will be hard pressed to meet its labor needs with its own citizens. In 1999, 28.6 percent of Hispanic youths and 12.6 percent of African American youths between the ages of 16 and 24 had dropped out of high school, compared to 7.3 percent of White youths and 11.2 percent of all youths (National Center for Education Statistics, 2001). There will be a mismatch between the skills of a large percentage of the workers in the United States and the needs of the labor force.

Scientific, technical, and service jobs will be ample, but the potential workers—about one-third of whom will be people of color—will not have the knowledge and skills to do the jobs. This will occur because of the increasingly large percentage of the school-age population that will be youths of color by 2020 (about 46 percent) and the low quality of the elementary and secondary education that a large number of youths of color are receiving. The problems that these students experience in the schools are summarized in the report, *Education That Works* (Quality Education for Minorities Project, 1990, pp. 11–12), a report published at the Massachusetts Institute of Technology:

> Many schools...continue to operate with outmoded curricula and structures based on the assumption that only a small elite will have or need to have substantial academic success. The problems our children face in and out of the classroom—racism, poverty, language differences, and cultural barriers—are not adequately addressed in today's typical school. We have had, consequently, low achievement and high dropout rates.

There will be an insufficient number of Whites, and particularly White males, to meet U.S. labor demands in the next few decades. Consequently, to meet workforce demands, women and people of color will have to enter scientific and technical fields in greater numbers. One out of three Ph.D.s awarded in the natural sciences and engineering in 1988 went to foreigners, compared with one in four in 1977. *Time* magazine wrote in its September 11, 1989, issue, "The science deficit threatens America's prosperity and possibly even its national security."

Whites are a diminishing percentage of new entrants to the U.S. labor force and of the nation's population because of the low birthrate among Whites and the small proportion of immigrants to the United States who are coming from Europe. In 1998, 56.7 percent of the documented immigrants to the United States came from Latin America (23.7 percent) and Asia (33 percent); and 14 percent came from Europe (U.S. Census Bureau, 2000, p. 10).

The United States is experiencing its largest wave of immigrants since the period from 1880 to 1924, when many Southern, Eastern, and Central European immigrants came to this land. About 1 million immigrants entered the United States each year during the peak years of the 1990s. Because of the low birthrate among Whites, the large influx of immigrants from Asia and Latin America, and the high birthrates among these groups, the White percentage of the U.S. population is experiencing very little growth. The White population in the United States grew about 4 percent between 1990 and 1999, compared to about 13 percent for African Americans, 40 percent for Hispanics, and 46 percent for Asians (U.S. Census Bureau, July, 1992; U.S. Census Bureau, November, 1992). Hispanics are one of the nation's fastest-growing groups. They increased from about 22 million in 1990 to more than 35 million in 2000 (U.S. Census Bureau, 2000).

In 1999, people of color made up 28.6 percent of the U.S. Population (U.S. Census Bureau, 2000). The growth in the nation's percentage of people of color is expected to outpace the growth in the percentage of Whites into the foreseeable future. The U.S. Census Bureau (2000) projects that Whites will constitute 52.5 percent of the nation's population in the year 2050, thus constituting only a small majority.

The Problem of Poverty and the Development of the Future Workforce

The gap between the relatively affluent 85 percent of U.S. society and the desperately poor 15 percent of the population continues to widen (Staff of *Fortune,* 1990). This gap is divided heavily along racial lines. Many African Americans and Latinos are trapped in low-income inner-city communities in which they not only have little contact with Whites, but they also have little contact and interaction with middle- and upper-status members of their own ethnic groups (Wilson, 1996).

The desertion of inner-city communities is not by Whites alone. Middle-class African Americans and Latinos have joined the exodus to the suburbs and to private schools. A salient characteristic of the United States today is a deepening social-class schism within—as well as across—ethnic and racial groups. Today, the flight out of the inner city is class based as well as racial. Consequently, a large group of low-income African American and Latino youths are socialized within communities in which they have little contact and interaction with middle-class individuals who belong to their own ethnic groups. These youths are often called the *underclass* by the popular media and social scientists. This term is considered pejorative by many people and may contribute to the further marginalization of these youths and their families.

Prior to the Civil Rights Movement of the 1960s and 1970s, and the open housing legislation that resulted from it, most middle-class African American and Latino professionals, such as teachers, lawyers, and social workers, lived in ethnic communities and served as important role models, mentors, and inspirational leaders for low-income ethnic youths. These ethnic professionals were confined to ethnic communities largely because of housing discrimination.

An increasing percentage of the nation's school-age youths are victims of poverty, as well as confined and isolated in low-income, inner-city communities. About one of every five children in the United States lives in poverty (Ford Foundation, 1989, p. 10). The proportion of children living in poverty is expected to increase in the years ahead, from about 21 percent of all children in 1984 to 27 percent of all children in 2020 (Pallas, Natriello, & McDill, 1989). The large number of American youths who are victims of poverty poses a serious problem for the development of effective citizens and workers. Youths who are victims of poverty are at a high risk of becoming school dropouts, experiencing academic failure, and engaging in antisocial behavior. It is very difficult for youths who drop out of school or who experience academic failure to become effective and productive citizens in a postindustrial, knowledge society.

School Reform

Restructuring Schools

An important implication of the demographic and social trends described above is that a major goal of education must be to help low-income students, linguistic minority students, and students of color to develop the knowledge, attitudes, and skills needed to participate in the mainstream workforce and in the mainstream society in the twenty-first century. This goal is essential but is not sufficient—nor is it possible to attain, in my view, without restructuring educational institutions and institutionalizing new goals and ideals within them. We must also rethink the goals of our society and nation-state if we are to become a strong, democratic, and just society.

I do not believe that our schools, as they are currently structured, conceptualized, and organized, will be able to help most students of color and linguistic minority students—especially those who are poor and from cultures that differ from the school culture in significant ways—to acquire the knowledge, attitudes, and skills needed to function effectively in the knowledge society of the next century. Our schools were designed for a different population, at a time when immigrant and poor youths did not need to be literate or have basic skills to get jobs and to become self-supporting citizens. When large numbers of immigrants entered the United States in the early 1900s, jobs in heavy industry were available that required little formal knowledge or skills. Thus, the school was less important as a job-preparatory institution.

To help our future citizens become effective and productive citizens in this century, our schools must be restructured. By restructuring, I mean a fundamental examination of the goals, values, and purposes of schools and a reconstruction of them. When restructuring occurs, the total system is recognized as the problem and is the target of reform (Darling-Hammond, 1997). Incremental and piecemeal changes are viewed as insufficient as a reform strategy.

To restructure schools, we need educational leaders who have a vision and who are transformative in orientation. In his influential book, *Leadership,* Burns (1978) identifies two types of leaders: *transformative* and *transactional.* Transformative leaders have a vision that they use to mobilize people to action. This is in contrast to transactional leadership, which is quid pro quo: "If you scratch my back, I will scratch yours." Transactional leadership, which is pervasive within our educational institutions and the larger society, is not motivating people to act and is not resulting in the kinds of changes that we need to respond to the demographic imperative described above. To respond to the demographic imperative, we need transformative leaders who have a vision of the future and the skills and abilities to communicate that vision to others.

Schools must help youths from diverse cultures and groups to attain the knowledge, attitudes, and skills needed to function effectively in this century. To attain this goal, the school must change many of its basic assumptions and practices. School restructuring is essential because the dominant approaches, techniques, and practices used to educate students do not, and I believe will not, succeed with large numbers of students of color, such as African Americans, Native Americans, and Latinos. Most current school practices are having little success with these students for many complex reasons, including negative perceptions and expectations of them that are held by many teachers and administrators. Many of the adults in the lives of these students have little faith in their ability, and many of the students—who have internalized these negative views—have little faith in themselves.

Many of these students are socialized in families and communities where they have seen a lot of failure, misery, and disillusionment. Many of them have seen or experienced little success, especially success that is related to schooling and education. One high school teacher asked a group of his students to write about their successes and failures. One of his Native American students told him that he could not write about success but that he could write easily and at length about failure because he had experienced so much of it. The student then wrote a poignant and moving essay about the daunting failures that he had experienced in his short life.

Increasing Academic Achievement

To help students of color and low-income students to experience academic success, and thus to become effective citizens, the school must be restructured so that these students will have successful experiences within a nurturing, personalized, and caring environment. Some fundamental reforms will have to occur in schools for this kind of environment to be created. Grouping practices that relegate a disproportionate number of low-income students and students of color to lower-tracked classes, in which they receive an inferior education, will have to be dismantled (Oakes, 1992). A norm will have to be institutionalized within the school that states that all students can and will learn, regardless of their home situations, race, social class, or ethnic group.

The theories and techniques developed by researchers such as Wilbur Brookover and his colleagues (1979); Ronald Edmonds (1986); and James P. Comer (1988) can help schools bring about the structural changes needed to implement the idea within a school that all children can and will learn. The significant work done in the effective schools movement during the 1970s and 1980s provide important lessons about the powerful role schools can play in increasing the academic achievement of low-income and minority students (Levine & Lezotte, 1995).

The whole-school reforms projects that have been implemented within the last two decades are also sources of rich ideas about ways to increase the academic and social achievement of students of color and low-income students. The whole-school reforms include Accelerated Schools; The Algebra Project, directed by Robert P. Moses; the Comer School Development Program; and Success for All, developed by Robert E. Slavin and his colleagues at Johns Hopkins University. An overview of these programs can be found on the Center for Multicultural Education (University of Washington) website: http://depts.washington.edu/centerme/home.htm. Another useful reference is a special issue of the *Journal of Education for Students Placed at Risk* (Boykin & Slavin, 2000).

Innovative ways need to be devised that involve joint parent-school effort in the education of ethnic and linguistic minority students. Most parents want their children to experience success in school, even though they may have neither the knowledge nor the resources to actualize their aspirations for their children. Successful educational interventions with low-income students and students of color are more likely to succeed if they have a parent-involvement component, as Comer (1988) has demonstrated with his successful interventions in inner-city, predominantly Black schools. Because of the tremendous changes that have occurred in U.S. families within the last two decades, we need to rethink and reconceptualize what parent involvement means and to formulate new ways to involve parents at a time when large numbers of school-age youths are from single-parent or two-working-parent families (C. A. M. Banks, 2001).

Empowering Teachers

To restructure schools in a way that increases their ability to educate low-income youths and youths of color, classroom teachers must be nurtured, empowered, and revitalized. Disempowered, alienated, underpaid, and disaffected teachers cannot help students who are victimized by poverty and discrimination to master the knowledge and skills they need to participate effectively in mainstream society in the twenty-first century.

Many of the teachers in U.S. schools—especially those who work in inner-city schools with large numbers of low-income students, students of color, and linguistic minority students—are victimized by societal forces similar to those that victimize their students. Many of these teachers are underpaid, held in low esteem by elites in society, treated with little respect by the bureaucratic and hierarchical school districts in which they work, victims of stereotypes, and blamed for many problems that are beyond their control. The standards movement, with its focus on high-stakes testing and accountability, has increased the sense of victimization felt by many teachers in the nation's inner-city and low-income schools (Heubert & Hauser, 1999; Kohn, 2000; Meir, 2000).

It is unreasonable to expect disempowered and victimized teachers to empower and motivate disaffected youths of color. Consequently, major goals of school restructuring must be to give teachers respect, to provide them the ability and authority to make decisions that matter, and to hold them accountable as professionals for the decisions they make. School reform will succeed only if we treat teachers in ways that we have long admonished them to treat their students. We must have high expectations for teachers, involve them genuinely in decision making, stop teacher bashing, and treat them in a caring and humane way. Only when teachers feel empowered and honored will they have the will and ability to treat students that society has victimized with respect and caring.

The Need for Societal Reform

Teachers and administrators should have the knowledge and skills needed to help students become change agents within society. Education should not just educate students to fit into the existing workforce and the current societal structure. Citizenship education in a multicultural society should have as an important goal helping all students to develop the knowledge, attitudes, and skills needed not only to participate within our society but also to help reform and reconstruct it. Problems such as racism, sexism, poverty, and inequality are widespread and permeate many of the nation's institutions, including the workforce, the courts, and the schools. To educate future citizens merely to fit into and not to change society will result in a perpetuation and escalation of these problems, including the widening gap between the rich and the poor, racial conflict and tension, and a growing number of people who are victims of poverty and homelessness.

A society that has sharp divisions between the rich and the poor, and between Whites and people of color, is not a stable one. It contains stresses and tensions that can lead to societal upheavals and racial polarization and conflict. Thus, education for the twenty-first century must not only help students to become literate and reflective citizens who can participate productively in the workforce but it must also teach them to care about other people in their communities and to take personal, social, and civic action to create a more humane and just society.

The Future

The demographic trends and projections described in this chapter indicate that the United States must act quickly to educate its low-income population and to preserve its rich linguistic and cultural resources, or face the future as a second-rate and declining nation. This is because the White population is aging and declining as a percentage of the total, while the population of people of color—especially Asians and Latinos—is growing by leaps and bounds. In the future, Whites will make up a disproportionate share of the nation's retirees, who will be heavily dependent on workers of color to support them through the Social Security Benefit system.

Poor children, children of color, and linguistic minority students are important parts of the future of the United States. The country's ultimate test as a nation will be not how it treats its citizens who are successful but how it responds to the desperate plight of those who are poor and undereducated. These citizens have the potential to contribute strength and compassion to the nation. There are some hopeful signs that an increasing number of Americans are beginning to realize that bold steps must be taken to educate its citizens of color and to educate all of its citizens to live in a multicultural society—not out of kindness for the downtrodden, but for national survival.

Intergroup Education

The previous section of this chapter focuses on the need for school reform to increase the academic achievement of all students, especially the achievement of students of color and low-income youth who experience many academic problems. Another important goal of multicultural education is to reduce prejudice among all students and to help them to develop more democratic attitudes, beliefs, and actions. This section describes the nature of children's racial attitudes, and guidelines for helping students to develop positive racial attitudes, beliefs, and actions.

The Nature of Children's Racial Attitudes and Identity

Teachers of young children often tell me that their students are not aware of racial differences and have no racial prejudices. However, research over a period that spans more than seventy years indicates that young children are aware of the racial differences within adult society (Lasker, 1929). Their racial attitudes mirror those of adults (Cross, 1991; Lasker, 1929; Stephan, 1999).

In a series of landmark studies published between 1939 and 1950, Kenneth and Mamie Clark (1939, 1950), working with African Americans aged three to seven, established a paradigm in racial attitude research that is still highly influential. Using brown and white dolls as stimuli, the Clarks established that young African American children have accurate knowledge about different racial groups, tend to prefer white to brown dolls, and often make incorrect racial self-identifications. The Clarks interpreted the tendencies of African American children to prefer white to brown dolls and to make incorrect racial self-identifications as expressions of negative self-esteem, low self-concept, identity confusion, and racial self-rejection.

During the 1950s and 1960s, a score of other researchers—working within the research paradigm established by the Clarks—confirmed the Clarks' findings (e.g., Goodman, 1952; Williams & Edwards, 1969). Most of this research also included preschool and kindergarten White children as subjects. It indicated that White children tend to make own-group preferences (tend to select white dolls) and, unlike African American children, tend to make correct racial self-identifications.

The Clarks' paradigm, which may be called the self-rejection hypothesis, dominated the social science and educational literature from the 1930s to the 1970s. Since the 1970s, however, the Clarks' paradigm has been seriously challenged by a number of researchers and theorists. The challenges to the Clarks' paradigm have taken several forms, including the search for different explanations of the pro-White bias exemplified by African American children, a few studies that have contradicted their findings, and arguments that describe the methodological weaknesses of the studies by the Clarks and their followers.

During the 1980s, researchers such as Spencer (1982, 1984) and Cross (1991) developed concepts, theories, and research that strongly challenged the notion that young African American children who express Eurocentric racial preferences have negative self-esteem, self-hate, and dysfunctional personalities. These researchers have made a useful conceptual distinction between *personal identity* (self-concept, self-esteem) and *group identity* or reference-group orientation.

In a series of pioneering studies, Spencer (1982, 1984) has marshaled significant support for the postulate that young African American children are able to distinguish their personal identity from their group identity, and can have high self-esteem and yet express a White bias. The expression of a White bias results from a cognitive process that enables young children to accurately perceive the norms and attitudes toward Whites and Blacks in U.S. society.

Banks and Banks (1983) studied the racial attitudes, preferences, and self-identifications of a sample of twenty-three preschool and kindergarten African American children who lived in the predominantly White suburban communities of a city in the Northwest. The children in this study had biracial attitudes. They liked both African Americans and Whites. Most of them believed that Blacks and Whites were equally good looking and equally good as students. However, they were slightly biased toward African Americans.

Previous investigators have assumed that psychologically healthy children should make own-group racial preferences. They have assumed this in large part because most White children, beginning at age four, make own-group racial preferences (Aboud, 1988). African American and Mexican American children tend to make in-group as well as out-group racial preferences, which I call *biracial* or *bicultural* preferences. Parents of color tend to socialize their children so that they will function effectively both in their ethnic communities and in the mainstream society.

There is almost no discussion in existing studies of the extent to which young children make biracial choices. These findings tend to be ignored or to be interpreted negatively because they are inconsistent with existing research paradigms. We live in a multicultural society. A research paradigm needs to be established that focuses on the bicultural and biracial choices that children make, that interprets the important differences within ethnic groups, and that assumes that bi-group preferences, rather than own-group preferences, are healthy and desirable within a multicultural society.

The Modification of Children's Racial Attitudes

In a comprehensive review of the research (Banks, 1993c), I identify four types of intervention studies that have been conducted to help children to develop more democratic racial attitudes and behaviors. These are laboratory reinforcement studies, perceptual differentiation studies, curricular intervention studies, and studies that use cooperative learning activities and contact situations. This research indicates that teachers can help students to develop more positive racial attitudes by designing and implementing well-planned and well-conceptualized curricular interventions.

In a series of laboratory studies conducted by Williams and Morland (1976) and their colleagues, researchers have been able to reduce White bias in both African American and White children by using reinforcement procedures. In one study (Williams & Edwards, 1969), for example, the investigators showed the children a white horse and a black horse, and a white figure and a brown figure. The researchers were able to reduce White bias in the students by giving them positive reinforcement when they chose positive—rather than negative—adjectives to describe the black horse and the brown figure. Researchers using reinforcement techniques have found that when White bias is reduced using black and white animals and boxes, the changed attitudes are generalized to human figures and photographs. It is important to point out that these interventions reduce but do not eliminate White bias in young children.

Katz and Zalk (1978) examined the effects of four different interventions on the racial attitudes of second- and fifth-grade children high in prejudice. The four interventions were perceptual differentiation of minority group faces, increased positive interracial contact, vicarious interracial contact, and reinforcement of the color black. The perceptual differentiation treatment was based on the hypothesis that people find it more difficult to differentiate the faces of members of out-groups than to differentiate the faces of members of their own groups. It is not uncommon to hear a member of one racial group say that he or she has trouble telling members of another group apart. Katz and Zalk hypothesized that if they could teach children to better differentiate the faces of out-groups, prejudice would be reduced. Each of the four interventions was effective in reducing prejudice. However, the vicarious contact and perceptual differentiation treatments had the most long-term effects.

A number of curriculum intervention studies that use multiethnic materials have been conducted. Trager and Yarrow (1952) found that first- and second-grade children who experienced a democratic, multicultural curriculum developed more positive racial attitudes than did students who experienced a traditional, mainstream curriculum. Litcher and Johnson (1969) found that multiethnic readers helped White second-grade children to develop more positive racial attitudes. However, when they replicated the study using photographs (Litcher, Johnson, & Ryan, 1973), the children's attitudes were not significantly changed. The Litcher, Johnson, and Ryan study highlights an important trend in the prejudice-reduction literature. Although curricular materials can help students develop more positive racial attitudes, successful intervention is a complicated process that is influenced by a number of factors, including the teacher's racial attitudes and skills, the length of the intervention, the classroom atmosphere, the ethnic and racial composition of the school and classroom, and the racial atmosphere and composition of the community.

Since 1970, a number of researchers have studied the effects of cooperative learning on the academic achievement and racial attitudes of students from different racial and ethnic groups (Aronson & Gonzalez, 1988; Slavin, 1995). This research has been heavily influenced by Allport's contact theory (1954). Allport hypothesized that prejudice would be reduced if interracial contact situations have the following characteristics:

1. They are cooperative rather than competitive.
2. The individuals experience equal status.
3. The contact is sanctioned by authorities such as parents, principals, and teachers.

The research on cooperative learning activities indicate that African American, Mexican American, and White students develop more positive racial attitudes and choose more friends from outside racial groups when they participate in group activities that have the conditions identified by Allport. Cooperative learning activities also have a positive effect on the academic achievement of students of color.

Guidelines for Reducing Prejudice in Students

The following guidelines are derived from the research discussed above as well as from two reviews of the research that I completed (Banks, 1991a, 1993c):

1. Include positive and realistic images of ethnic and racial groups in teaching materials in a consistent, natural, and integrated fashion.
2. Help children to differentiate the faces of members of outside racial and ethnic groups. The best way to do this is to permeate the curriculum with different faces of members of these groups.
3. Involve children in vicarious experiences with various racial and ethnic groups. For example, use films, videos, children's books, recordings, photographs, and other kinds of vicarious experiences to expose children to members of different racial and ethnic groups. Vicarious experiences are especially important for students in predominantly White, Latino, or African American schools or communities who do not have much direct contact with members of other racial, ethnic, and social-class groups. Research indicates that vicarious experiences can be powerful (Katz & Zalk, 1978; Litcher & Johnson, 1969). However, vicarious experiences with different ethnic and racial groups should acquaint students with many different types of people within these groups.

4. If you teach in an interracial school, involve children in structured interracial contact situations. However, contact alone does not necessarily help children to develop positive racial attitudes. Effective interracial contact situations must have the characteristics described by Allport (1954).
5. Provide positive verbal and nonverbal reinforcement for the color brown.
6. Involve children from different racial and ethnic groups in cooperative learning activities.

Preparing Students for a Changing, Diverse, and Complex World

The demographic changes that are taking place in the United States make it essential for teachers and administrators to (1) restructure schools so that students from all ethnic, racial, gender, and social-class groups will have an equal opportunity to learn; and (2) implement prejudice-reduction strategies so that all students will develop the knowledge, attitudes, and skills needed to function in an increasingly diverse, tense, and problem-ridden world. Because of the enormous problems within our nation and world, educators cannot be neutral (Edelman, 1992). They can either act to help transform our world or enhance the escalation of our problems by inaction. Each educator must make a choice. What will be yours?

CHAPTER

5 Knowledge Components

Eight characteristics of the multicultural school are described in Chapter 2 (see Table 2.1). Each of these elements must be reformed in order to enable schools to create equal educational opportunities for all students and to help students develop the knowledge, skills, and attitudes needed to function effectively in a changing national and world society. One of the eight characteristics of an effective multicultural school identified in Table 2.1 is positive teacher attitudes and behaviors. To acquire the attitudes, perceptions, and behavior needed to actualize multicultural education in their schools, teachers need a sound knowledge base in multicultural education. This chapter describes the knowledge that teachers need to master in order to be effective in multicultural classrooms and schools.

The Four Knowledge Categories

To become effective multicultural teachers, teachers need the following:

1. *Knowledge of the major paradigms* in multicultural education
2. *Knowledge of the major concepts* in multicultural education
3. *Historical and cultural knowledge* of the major ethnic groups
4. *Pedagogical knowledge* about how to adapt curriculum and instruction to the unique needs of students from diverse cultural, ethnic, and social-class groups

This chapter focuses on the first three categories of knowledge. Chapter 6 describes pedagogical knowledge.

Multicultural Education Paradigms

A paradigm is an interrelated set of ideas that explain human behavior or a phenomenon. It implies policy and action and has specific goals, assumptions, and values. Paradigms compete with one another in the arena of ideas and public policy.

Since the 1960s, several major paradigms have been formulated explaining why many low-income students and students of color have low levels of academic achievement (Banks, 2001; Banks & Banks, 1995). Two of these paradigms or explanations are the *cultural deprivation* paradigm and the *cultural difference* paradigm. These two paradigms have very different assumptions, research findings, and implications for teaching in multicultural classrooms. Teachers who embrace the cultural deprivation paradigm and those who embrace the cultural difference paradigm are likely to respond to low-income students and students of color differently in classroom interactions and to have different ideas about how to increase their academic achievement. See Banks (2001) for a discussion of other paradigms. A fuller discussion of the cultural deprivation and cultural difference paradigms follows.

The Cultural Deprivation Paradigm. Cultural deprivation theorists assume that low-income students do not achieve well in school because of the culture of poverty in which they are socialized. These theorists believe that characteristics such as poverty, disorganized families, and single-parent homes cause children from low-income communities to experience "cultural deprivation" and "irreversible cognitive deficits."

Cultural deprivationists assume that a major goal of the school is to provide "culturally deprived" students with the cultural and other experiences that will compensate for their cognitive and intellectual deficits. These theorists believe that low-income students can learn the basic skills taught by the schools, but that these skills must be taught using behaviorist methods and strategies.

Cultural deprivation theorists see the major problem as the culture of the students rather than the culture of the school. Teachers and administrators who embrace the cultural deprivation paradigm often blame the victims for their problems and academic failure. They assume that low-income students and students of color often do poorly in school because of their cultural and social-class characteristics, not because they are ineffectively taught. They believe that the school is limited in what it can do to help these students achieve because of the culture into which they are socialized. Advocates of this paradigm focus on changing the student rather than on changing the culture of the school to enable it to focus on the cultural strengths of students from diverse social-class and ethnic groups.

The Cultural Difference Paradigm. Unlike the cultural deprivation theorists, cultural difference theorists reject the idea that low-income students and students of color have cultural deficits. They believe that ethnic groups such as African Americans, Mexican Americans, Asian Americans, and Native Americans have strong, rich, and diverse cultures

(Gay, 2000; Lomawaima, 1995). These cultures consist of languages, values, behavioral styles, and perspectives that can enrich the lives of all Americans. Low-income students and students of color fail to achieve in school not because they have culturally deprived cultures but because their cultures are different from the culture of the school and the mainstream culture most valued by society (Ladson-Billings, 1994).

Cultural difference theorists believe that the school, rather than the cultures of low-income students and students of color, is primarily responsible for the low academic achievement of low-income students and students of color (González et al., 1993; Mehan, Villanueva, Hubbard, & Lintz, 1996; Tharp, Estrada, Dalton, & Yamauchi, 2000). The school must change in ways that will allow it to respect and reflect the cultures of low-income students and students of color and at the same time use teaching strategies that are consistent with their cultural characteristics. Culturally sensitive and enriched teaching strategies will motivate low-income students and students of color and will enable them to achieve at high levels (Boykin, 2000). The schools, argue cultural difference theorists, often fail to help low-income students and students of color to achieve because schools frequently ignore or try to alienate them from their cultures and rarely use teaching strategies that are consistent with their lifestyles. Cultural difference theorists frequently cite research that shows how the culture of the school and the cultures of low-income students and students of color differ in values, norms, and behaviors (Heath, 1983; Hollins, 1996; Ladson-Billings, 1994; Ramirez & Castañeda, 1974).

Much of the research developed by cultural difference theorists focuses on the language and learning style of students of color. Linguists such as Roger Shuy, William Labov, Joan Baratz (Williams, 1970), and Geneva Smitherman (2000) have described Black English, or Ebonics (the version of English spoken by many African Americans), as a rich version of English that is logical, consistent in style and usage, and very effective in communicating a sense of kinship and unity among African Americans. Many teachers, however, view Black English negatively. Sociolinguists urge teachers to view Black English from a positive perspective and to use it as a vehicle to help its speakers to learn Standard English as an alternative dialect, not as a replacement for their first language (Delpit, 1997; Perry & Delpit, 1998). Cultural difference theorists also advise teachers to view other languages spoken by their students, such as Spanish and Vietnamese, as strengths rather than as problems to be overcome (August & Hakuta, 1997; Minami & Kennedy, 1992; Ovando & Collier, 1998).

Research by cultural difference theorists such as Hale-Benson (1986), Shade, Kelly & Oberg (1997), Ramírez and Castañeda (1974), Philips (1983), Vogt, Jordan, and Tharp (1987), Delpit (1988), Irvine (1990), and Ladson-Billings (1990; 1994) indicate that most African American, Hispanic, Native American, and Native Hawaiian students have some learning and cultural characteristics that are inconsistent with the school culture.

This research indicates, for example, that Mexican American students tend to be more field-sensitive than do mainstream White students. The learning and affective characteristics of field-sensitive and field-independent students differ in a number of significant ways (Ramírez & Castañeda, 1974). Field-sensitive students tend to like to work with others to achieve a common goal. They are more sensitive to the feelings and opinions of others than are field-independent students, who prefer to work independently and to compete and gain individual recognition.

Learning style theory is often misinterpreted and misused by teachers and other school practitioners (Irvine & York, 1995). It is often interpreted to mean that if a student is Latino or African American, he or she will have a field-sensitive learning style. This kind of thinking results in the formation of new stereotypes about students from diverse racial and ethnic groups. Although some groups of African American and Latino students are more likely to have field-sensitive learning characteristics than are some groups of mainstream Anglo students, all kinds of learning styles are found among all groups of students. Educators should keep the complexity of group characteristics in mind when they read studies or theories about learning styles. Learning style theory is harmful when it is oversimplified by teachers and other school practitioners.

Research on the effects of cooperative learning techniques by Slavin (1983; 1995) and Aronson and Gonzalez (1988) provides some support for learning styles theories. These researchers have found that the academic achievement of Latino and African American students is enhanced when they are taught using cooperative learning strategies. This research also indicates that both White students and students of color develop more positive racial attitudes when they participate in cooperative learning situations and tasks.

Concepts in Multicultural Education

Concepts are important ideas that scientists use to classify and categorize information, data, and ideas (see Chapter 6). The heart of a discipline or field of study is its key concepts, generalizations, and principles. Culture is a major concept in multicultural education. We now examine culture and two related concepts: *macroculture* and *microculture.*

Culture. There are many different definitions of culture, but no single definition that all social scientists would heartily accept. Culture can be defined as the way of life of a social group—the total human-made environment (Berger, 1995; Geertz, 1995). Although culture is often defined in a way that includes all the material and nonmaterial aspects of group life, most social scientists today emphasize the intangible, symbolic, and ideational aspect of culture.

It is the values, symbols, interpretations, and perspectives that distinguish one people from another in modernized societies, and not artifacts, material objects, and other tangible aspects of human societies. Values, norms, and perspectives distinguish ethnic groups such as Native Americans, African Americans, and Jewish Americans rather than the foods they eat or the clothes they wear. The essence of an ethnic culture in a modernized society such as the United States is its unique values, beliefs, symbols, and perspectives. Consequently, when teachers teach about groups such as Native Americans and Mexican Americans by having the students build teepees or eat tacos, they have missed the essence of the cultures of these groups and given the students misleading and distorted conceptions of their cultures.

Cultures are dynamic, complex, and changing. When teaching about the cultures of groups such as African Americans, Jewish Americans, and Japanese Americans, the teacher should be careful to help students to understand how such factors as time of immigration, social class, region, religion, gender, exceptionality, and education influence the behaviors and values of both individuals and subgroups within an ethnic group. An East Coast, upper-middle-class, college-educated Chicana (Mexican American female) whose family has been in the United States since the turn of the century will differ in significant ways from a male Mexican migrant worker in California who has lived in the United States less than two decades.

Teachers should help students to understand the complex characteristics of ethnic groups in order to prevent students from developing new stereotypes when ethnic groups are studied in school. Any discussion of the general characteristics of an ethnic group must be mediated by a consideration of how individual members of the group may differ from the group norms and characteristics in significant ways. Table 5.1 describes some of the key variables on which individuals within an ethnic or cultural group may differ.

Macroculture and Microculture. The concept of culture as formulated by most social scientists does not deal with variations within the national culture or the smaller cultures within it. However, when dealing with multicultural education, it is necessary to describe variations within the national culture because multicultural education focuses on equal educational opportunities for different groups within the national culture. Two related concepts can help us deal with cultural variation within the national culture. We can call the national or shared culture of the

TABLE 5.1 Variables within Ethnic Groups on Which Individuals Differ

Variables	Understandings and Behavior	Levels of Competency
		1 2 3 4 5 6 7
Values and Behavioral Styles	The ability to understand and interpret values and behavioral styles that are normative within the ethnic group.	←——→
	The ability to express values behaviorally that are normative within the ethnic group.	
	The ability to express behavioral styles and nuances that are normative within the ethnic group.	
Languages and Dialects	The ability to understand, interpret, and speak the dialects and/or languages within the ethnic culture.	←——→
Nonverbal Communications	The ability to understand and accurately interpret the nonverbal communications within the ethnic group.	←——→
	The ability to communicate accurately nonverbally within the ethnic group.	
Cultural Cognitiveness	The ability to perceive and recognize the unique components of one's ethnic group that distinguishes it from other microcultural groups within the society and from the national macroculture.	←——→
	The ability to take actions that indicate an awareness and knowledge of one's ethnic culture.	
Perspectives, Worldviews, and Frames of Reference	The ability to understand and interpret the perspectives, worldviews, and frames of reference normative within the ethnic group.	←——→
	The ability to view events and situations form the perspectives, worldviews, and frames of reference normative within the ethnic group.	

TABLE 5.1 Continued

Variables	Understandings and Behavior	Levels of Competency
		1 2 3 4 5 6 7
Identification	The ability to have an identification with one's ethnic group that is subtle and/or unconscious. The ability to take overt actions that show conscious identification with one's ethnic group.	◄——————►

Source: Reprinted with permission from James A. Banks (2001). *Cultural Diversity and Education: Foundations, Curriculum and Teaching* (4th edition). Boston: Allyn and Bacon, p. 82.

nation-state or society the big culture, or *macroculture*. The smaller cultures that constitute it can be called *microcultures*.

Every nation-state has overarching values, symbols, and ideations that are to some degree shared by all microcultures. Various microcultural groups within the nation, however, may mediate, interpret, reinterpret, perceive, and experience these overarching national values and ideals differently.

The national, overarching ideals, symbols, and values can be described for various nation-states. Myrdal (1944), the Swedish economist, identifies values such as justice, equality, and human dignity as overarching values in the United States. He calls these the American creed values. Myrdal also describes the "American dilemma" as an integral part of U.S. society. This dilemma results from the fact that even though most U.S. citizens internalize American creed values, such as justice and human dignity, they often violate them in their daily behavior. Myrdal concludes that a tremendous gap exists between American democratic ideals and American realities, such as racism and sexism. Other U.S. overarching values include the Protestant work ethic, individualism as opposed to group orientation, distance, and materialism and material progress.

Historical and Cultural Knowledge of Ethnic Groups

Teachers need a sound knowledge of the history and culture of ethnic groups in order to successfully integrate ethnic content into the school curriculum (Banks, 1997b; Franklin & Moss, 1988; Gutierrez, 1995; Rodriguez, 1989; Takaki, 1989). However, factual knowledge about ethnic groups is necessary but not sufficient. This knowledge needs to be organized and taught with key concepts (e.g., powerful ideas), themes, and issues in the experiences of ethnic and cultural groups. The experiences of ethnic groups in the United States can be viewed and compared by using several powerful key concepts and ideas. I describe eleven key concepts and discuss how each can be used to view and study the experiences of selected ethnic groups. These eleven key concepts are summarized in Table 5.2. Chapter 6 contains teaching units that describe how to teach two of these concepts: *knowledge construction* and *revolution.*

Key Concepts for Studying the Experiences of Ethnic and Cultural Groups

1. *Origins and immigration.* When studying about an ethnic group in the United States, it is important to examine its origins and immigration patterns. Most groups in the United States came from other lands. However, archeologists believe that Native Americans entered North America by crossing the Bering Strait between 40,000 and 45,000 years ago (Snipp, 1989). However, when studying about the origins of the first Americans, it is important to point out to students that many Native Americans believe that they were created in this land by the Great Spirit (Champagne, 1994). Both perspectives on the origins of Native Americans should be presented and respected in the multicultural classroom.

The ancestors of the Mexican Americans are also natives to the Americas. A new people were created when the Spanish conquistadors and the Indians of the Americas produced offspring, who were called *mestizos.* When the United States acquired about one-third of Mexico's territory at the end of the United States–Mexican War in 1848, about 80,000 Mexicans became U.S. citizens (Gonzales, 1999). Today, about

TABLE 5.2 Key Concepts to Guide the Study of Ethnic and Cultural Groups

1. Origins and immigration
2. Shared culture, values, and symbols
3. Ethnic identity and sense of peoplehood
4. Perspectives, worldviews, and frames of reference
5. Ethnic institutions and self-determination
6. Demographic, social, political, and economic status
7. Prejudice, discrimination, and racism
8. Intraethnic diversity
9. Assimilation and acculturation
10. Revolution
11. Knowledge construction

half of the growth in the Mexican population results from immigration; the other half is from new births (U.S. Census Bureau, 1994).

2. *Shared culture, values, and symbols.* Most ethnic groups in the United States, especially ethnic groups of color, have unique cultures and values that resulted from an interaction of their original culture with the host culture in the United States, from ethnic institutions created partly as a response to discrimination, and from their social-class status. These cultures are still in the process of formation and change. Consequently, they are complex and dynamic. They cannot and should not be viewed as static.

Examples of unique values and cultures of ethnic groups include the strong family orientation of Italian Americans (McGoldrick, Giordano, & Pearce, 1996), the strong identity with their tribe and kinship group among Native Americans (Allen, 1986; Hirschfelder, 1995), and the group orientation of African Americans (White & Parham, 1990). Black English, a version of English spoken by many African Americans, is also an example of an ethnic cultural characteristic (Heath, 1983; Smitherman, 2000).

3. *Ethnic identity and sense of peoplehood.* A shared sense of peoplehood and ethnic identity is one of the most important characteristics of ethnic groups in the United States (Gordon, 1964). This shared sense of identity results from a common history and current experiences. Ethnic groups tend to view themselves and to be viewed by others as separate and apart from other groups in society. In the case of ethnic groups of color, such as African Americans and Mexican Americans, their shared sense of identity and peoplehood is reinforced by the racial discrimination they experience. The shared sense of identity of an ethnic group can and often does extend beyond national boundaries. Most Jews in New York and London share feelings about the Holocaust (Dershowitz, 1997; Jacoby, 2000). Most African Americans strongly identify with the struggle of the Blacks in South Africa.

4. *Perspectives, worldviews, and frames of reference.* Members of the same ethnic group often view reality in a similar way and differently from other groups within a society. This results largely from their shared sense of peoplehood and identity previously described. Most Latinos in the United States tend to have positive views toward bilingual education and believe that their children should be able to speak both Spanish and English (Crawford, 1989). However, because Latinos in the United States have diverse histories, origins, and social classes, there is a range of views on every issue within Latino communities, including bilingual education. Two noted Latinos who express conservative views on a range of issues, including bilingual education, are Richard Rodriguez (1982) and Linda Chavez (1991).

5. *Ethnic institutions and self-determination.* Many ethnic institutions were formed by groups in the United States in response to discrimination and segregation. Examples are African American churches,

schools, colleges, and insurance companies; and Japanese and Jewish social organizations. Many of these institutions continue to exist today because they help ethnic groups to satisfy unique social, cultural, and educational needs. Other ethnic institutions, such as the National Association for the Advancement of Colored People, the Anti-Defamation League of B'nai B'rith, the League of United Latin-American Citizens, and the Japanese American Citizenship League, were formed to work for the civil rights of specific ethnic groups and to fight discrimination.

6. *Demographic, social, political, and economic status.* When acquiring knowledge about ethnic groups in the United States, their current demographic, social, political, and economic status needs to be determined. The economic profile of Filipino Americans was one of the lowest in the United States in the 1960s. However, they now have a high economic status, primarily because of the large number of professional workers that immigrated to the United States from the Philippines during the 1970s and 1980s (Daniels, 1988; Takaki, 1989). The number of Asians and Pacific Islanders in the United States increased from 6.9 million in 1990 to 10.1 million in 1999, a 46 percent increase, compared to a 40 percent increase for Hispanics, a 13.1 percent increase for African Americans, a 4 percent increase for Whites, and a 8.6 percent increase for the total U.S. population. In 1999, the Asian and Pacific Islander population of the United States was 10,186,000 (U. S. Census Bureau, 2000). In 2000, the U.S. total population reached a record 281, 421, 906 (Holmes, 2000).

The economic and educational status of an ethnic group can change. For example, there was significant improvement in the economic and educational status of African Americans and Hispanics during the 1960s and 1970s. However, during the 1980s these groups lost ground in both economic and educational status. Although they experienced gains during the 1990s, the poverty rates among African Americans and Hispanics are still significantly higher than among Whites. In 1998, 10.5 percent of Whites, 25.6 percent of Hispanics, 26.1 percent of African Americans, and 12.7 percent of all races lived below the poverty level (U.S. Census Bureau, 2000).

7. *Prejudice, discrimination, and racism.* Whenever groups with different racial, ethnic, and cultural characteristics interact, ethnocentrism, discrimination, and racism develop (Hannaford, 1996; Omi & Winant, 1994). When discrimination based on race becomes institutionalized within a society and the dominant group has the power to implement its racial ideology within these institutions, institutional racism exists. Groups such as African Americans, Native Americans, Asian Americans, and Latinos have been historically—and are today—victims of institutional racism in the United States. However, racism today is much more subtle and less blatant than it was prior to the Civil Rights Movement of the 1960s and 1970s (Cose, 1993; Feagin & Sikes, 1994). Some of the most

blatant forms were eradicated during that period, largely in response to the Civil Rights Movement.

Prejudice, discrimination, and racism are important concepts for understanding the experiences of ethnic groups in the past, present, and future, not only in the United States but also in nations throughout the world (Hannaford, 1996).

8. *Intraethnic diversity.* Even though ethnic groups share a culture, values, a sense of identity, and a common history, there are tremendous differences within ethnic groups. These important differences must always be kept in mind when we study an ethnic group (see Table 5.1). If not, we may create new stereotypes and misconceptions. These differences result from such factors as region (e.g., whether rural or urban), social class, religion, age, gender, sexual orientation, and political affiliation. While it is important to recognize that ethnic groups share many important characteristics, keep in mind that we are describing groups, not individuals. An individual may embrace all or hardly any of the dominant characteristics of his or her ethnic group. This individual may also have a strong or a weak identity with his or her ethnic group.

9. *Assimilation and acculturation.* When an ethnic or cultural group assimilates, it gives up its characteristics and adopts those of another group (Gordon, 1964). Acculturation describes the process that occurs when the characteristics of a group are changed because of interaction with another cultural or ethnic group. When acculturation occurs, the interacting groups exchange cultural characteristics; thus, both are changed in the process.

Assimilation and acculturation are important for understanding the experiences of ethnic groups in the United States and the world. In most societies, the dominant ethnic or cultural group expects other groups to adopt its language, culture, values, and behavior. Moreover, the dominant group within a society is usually at least partially successful is getting other groups to adapt its culture and values because of the power that it exercises. Cultural conflict usually develops within modernized societies when ethnic minority groups hold on to many of their important cultural characteristics or when they are denied full participation in the dominant society after they have largely culturally assimilated. The dominant cultural group within a society, such as the Anglo-Saxon Protestants in the United States, often adopt cultural traits from ethnic groups of color, such as African Americans and Native Americans, without acknowledging them or giving them appropriate public recognition. The contributions that African Americans and Native Americans have made to American literature, government, and music are rarely acknowledged fully (Weatherford, 1992).

10. *Revolution.* A political revolution occurs when a fundamental change takes place in the leadership of a society (Marshall, 1994), usually through violent upheaval and armed conflict. Other basic changes within a society, which often take place over a long period of time, are also described as revolutions, such as the industrial and agricultural revolutions. These latter revolutions are gradual transformations of a society rather than sudden changes. Revolution is an important concept for understanding the history of most ethnic groups in the United States because of the influence of revolutions on their past. Revolution is also an important concept in the history of ethnic groups in the United States because the ideas related to it—such as oppression, alienation, and hope for change—have been decisive in the history of U.S. ethnic groups.

In 1680, an important American revolution occurred when the Pueblo Indians in New Spain (New Mexico) rebelled against their Spanish conquerors. The revolution was not successful in the long run because the Pueblos were eventually reconquered by the Spaniards with deadly vengeance.

Students need to view the revolution in the British colonies from a multicultural perspective to fully understand it because it had different meanings for different groups such as the Anglo Loyalists, the Anglo Revolutionaries, the various Native American groups, and the African Americans. Some ethnic groups fled in search of freedom in the United States after revolutions occurred in their native lands. When Castro took control of Cuba in 1959, thousands of Cubans sought refuge in the United States. The Cuban refugees who came to the United States during and in the years following the Castro revolution constitute the bedrock of the Cuban American community (Olson & Olson, 1995).

11. *Knowledge construction.* When studying the history and contemporary experiences of ethnic and cultural groups in the United States, it is important for students to understand how knowledge and interpretations are constructed. They also need to understand how cultural experiences, biases, and values influence the knowledge construction process (Banks, 1996c; Harding, 1991). A transformative, multicultural curriculum also helps students to construct their own interpretations. The constructivist approach to teaching and learning is a key component of the transformative, multicultural curriculum.

When teachers engage students in knowledge construction, the students are given opportunities to participate in building knowledge and to construct their own interpretations of historical, social, and current events. The knowledge construction approach to teaching is constructivist in orientation and is influenced by the work of the Russian psychologist Lev S. Vygotsky (Kozulin, 1986).

Knowledge construction is influenced significantly by the group experience of the knower. The knowledge constructed within a group is incorporated into the group's legends, myths, heroes, and heroines, and it reflects the group's values and beliefs. For example, the Battle of Little Big

Horn can be viewed as a noble defense of one's homeland (the Native American version) or as a vicious massacre of soldiers who were protecting Anglo American pioneers (the dominant Anglo American view at the time) (Garcia, 1993).

Knowledge construction is a powerful idea in multicultural education because it can be taught in all disciplines and content areas. It can be used to help students understand the values and assumptions that underlie the base-ten number system in mathematics, the scientific method in the natural and biological sciences, and literary interpretations in the language arts and humanities. Knowledge construction is also a powerful idea that can guide the development of activities and teaching strategies that will enable students to build their own interpretations of the past, present, and future.

CHAPTER

6 Teaching with Powerful Ideas

Can you list all of the major battles that occurred during the American Revolution or name each of the fifty state capitals? If you are like most people, you can't. Research indicates that people forget a very large percentage of the facts they learn (Greeno, Collins, & Resnick, 1996). What most people remember about the American Revolution is not all of the major battles that occurred but the major reasons the Revolution took place and what happened when it ended.

Most people can remember that many state capitals are located in smaller cities rather than in the largest city within a state. Albany, rather than New York City, is the capital of New York; Springfield is the capital of Illinois, not Chicago; Olympia is the capital of Washington, not Seattle.

People tend to remember big, powerful ideas rather than factual details. Big ideas are not only remembered longer but they also help people to gain a better understanding of events and phenomena, to categorize and classify observations, and to transfer knowledge from one situation to another.

The Conceptual Approach

The big, powerful ideas that people tend to remember and that facilitate understanding and transfer of knowledge are called *concepts* and *generalizations* (Banks & Banks, 1999). In the conceptual approach to teaching, the curriculum as well as units and lessons are organized around key concepts and generalizations from the various disciplines and subject areas. These powerful ideas help students to organize and synthesize large amounts of data and information (Taba, Durkin, Fraenkel, & McNaughton, 1971).

The Categories of Knowledge

In order to develop and teach a multicultural curriculum that focuses on powerful concepts and ideas, you need to understand the knowledge cat-

TABLE 6.1 The Categories of Knowledge

Concept: *Social Protest*

Fact: On February 1, 1960, the sit-in movement designed to end racially segregated accommodation facilities began when a group of African American students sat down at a lunch counter reserved for Whites at a Woolworth's store in Greensboro, North Carolina.

Lower-Level Generalization: The sit-in movement, boycotts, and the Black Power movement were part of a larger movement in the 1960s and 1970s whose goal was to end institutionalized racism and discrimination.

Intermediate-Level Generalization: The Civil Rights Movement in the United States spread as women, people with disabilities, and gays and lesbians started organized movements to end discrimination against their respective groups.

High-Level/Universal Generalization: When a group perceives itself as oppressed and believes that there is a possibility for a change and reform, it will initiate organized protest and resistance.

egories and their interrelationships: facts, concepts, and generalizations (Banks, 1991b). *Facts* are low-level, specific empirical statements. *Concepts* are words or phrases that enable people to categorize or classify a large class of observations and thus to reduce the complexity of their world. *Generalizations* are tested or verified statements that contain two or more concepts and state how they are related. Table 6.1 contains examples of these knowledge categories.

The treatment of concepts and generalizations is succinct in this book because of its brevity. Readers who would like a more detailed discussion of the knowledge categories as well as historical overviews of the major U.S. ethnic groups should see *Teaching Strategies for Ethnic Studies* (Banks, 1997b).

A Conceptual Multicultural Curriculum

To build a conceptual, multicultural curriculum, it is necessary to choose higher-level powerful concepts such as *culture, power, socialization, protest,* and *values* as organizing concepts. One of the best conceptual curriculums was developed by Hilda Taba and her colleagues (Taba, Durkin, Fraenkel, & McNaughton, 1971). It is a social studies curriculum designed for grades 1 through 8. The Taba Social Studies Curriculum is organized around these powerful, organizing concepts:

Causality
Conflict
Cooperation
Cultural change
Differences
Interdependence
Modification
Power
Societal control
Tradition
Values

Powerful organizing concepts for an interdisciplinary multicultural curriculum may be discipline specific, such as *culture* from anthropology and *socialization* from sociology. They may also be interdisciplinary, such as *modification* and *causality,* used in the Taba Social Studies Curriculum.

How to Develop a Multicultural Conceptual Curriculum

1. *Identify key concepts, such as ethnic diversity, immigration, and assimilation, around which you will organize your curriculum.* When choosing concepts around which to organize your curriculum, lessons, or units, keep these criteria in mind:

   a. The concepts should be powerful ones that can be used to organize a large quantity and scope of data and information.
   b. The concepts should be ones that can be used to organize and classify information from a range of disciplines and subject areas, such as the social sciences, literature and the language arts, and, when possible, the physical, natural, and biological sciences. Ethnic diversity is such a concept (see Table 6.2).
   c. Consider the developmental level of your students, in terms of their chronological age, cognitive development, moral development, and their prior experiences with ethnic and cultural content. *Prejudice* and *discrimination* are much more appropriate concepts to teach young children than is *racism.*

   Taba and her colleagues (1971, p. 28) recommend that the first four questions guide the selection of key concepts for a conceptual curriculum. I added the fifth question.

   (1) *Validity:* Do they adequately represent concepts of the disciplines from which they are drawn?
   (2) *Significance:* Can they explain important segments of the world today, and are they descriptive of important aspects of human behavior?
   (3) *Durability:* Are they of lasting importance?
   (4) *Balance:* Do they permit development of student thinking in both scope and depth?

TABLE 6.2 Teaching Ethnic Diversity in All Subject Areas

Key Concept: *Ethnic Diversity*

Key or Organizing Generalization: Most societies are characterized by ethnic diversity.

Intermediate-Level Generalization: Ethnic diversity is an important characteristic of the United States.

Lower-Level Generalizations:

Social Studies

The new wave of immigration to the United States since the 1960s has increased ethnic diversity within it.

Language Arts

Ethnic diversity is reflected in the variety of language and communication patterns in the United States.

Music

Ethnic diversity in the United States is reflected in its folk, gospel, and popular music.

Drama

The plays written by U.S. authors of varying ethnic backgrounds have enriched the national culture.

Physical and Movement Education

Dance and other forms of expressive movements in the United States reflect the nation's ethnic diversity.

Art

The visual arts in the United States reflect the nation's rich ethnic makeup.

Home Economics and Family Living

Ethnic diversity in the United States is reflected in the nation's foods and family life-styles.

Science

The diverse physical characteristics of the people in the United States reinforce ethnic diversity.

Mathematics

Mathematical notations and systems in the United States reflect the contributions of many different ethnic, racial, and cultural groups. This is rarely recognized.

(5) *Ethnic and cultural relevance:* Do they help students to better understand the experiences of ethnic groups in the United States and the world?

2. *Identify key or universal generalizations related to each of the key concepts chosen.*
3. *Identify an intermediate-level generalization for each of the key concepts.*
4. *Identify a lower-level generalization related to the key generalization for each of the subject areas in which the key concept will be taught.* The multicultural conceptual curriculum is interdisciplinary. Concepts are selected that can be used to incorporate information and data from several disciplines. In the example in Table 6.2, *ethnic diversity* is taught in each subject area. In actual practice, the concepts are likely to be taught in only two or three subject areas at the same time. Interdisciplinary teaching often requires team planning and teaching at the middle school level and beyond. Table 6.2 shows ethnic diversity being taught in each subject area to illustrate the powerful potential of the conceptual approach to teaching.
5. *Formulate teaching strategies and activities to teach the concepts and generalizations.* Teaching strategies for these two concepts are described in the second part of this chapter: (1) *the construction of historical knowledge* and (2) *revolutions.*

The Spiral Development of Concepts and Generalizations

In a conceptual, multicultural curriculum, the key concepts and generalizations identified are taught and developed at an increasing degree of complexity and depth throughout the grades. New content samples are used at each subsequent grade level to help the students learn the concepts and generalizations at an increasing degree of depth and complexity. Figure 6.1 illustrates how *social protest,* a concept, is introduced in grade 5 and is taught with increasing depth and complexity through grade 12.

Social Science and Value Inquiry Skills

It is very important for students to master facts, concepts, and generalizations, but it is just as important, if not more so, for them to gain proficiency in the processes involved in gathering and evaluating knowledge, identifying the biases and assumptions that underlie knowledge claims, and constructing knowledge themselves. An important goal of the multicultural curriculum is to help students develop proficiency in inquiry and thinking skills, such as stating research questions and problems, hypothesizing, conceptualizing, collecting and analyzing data, and deriv-

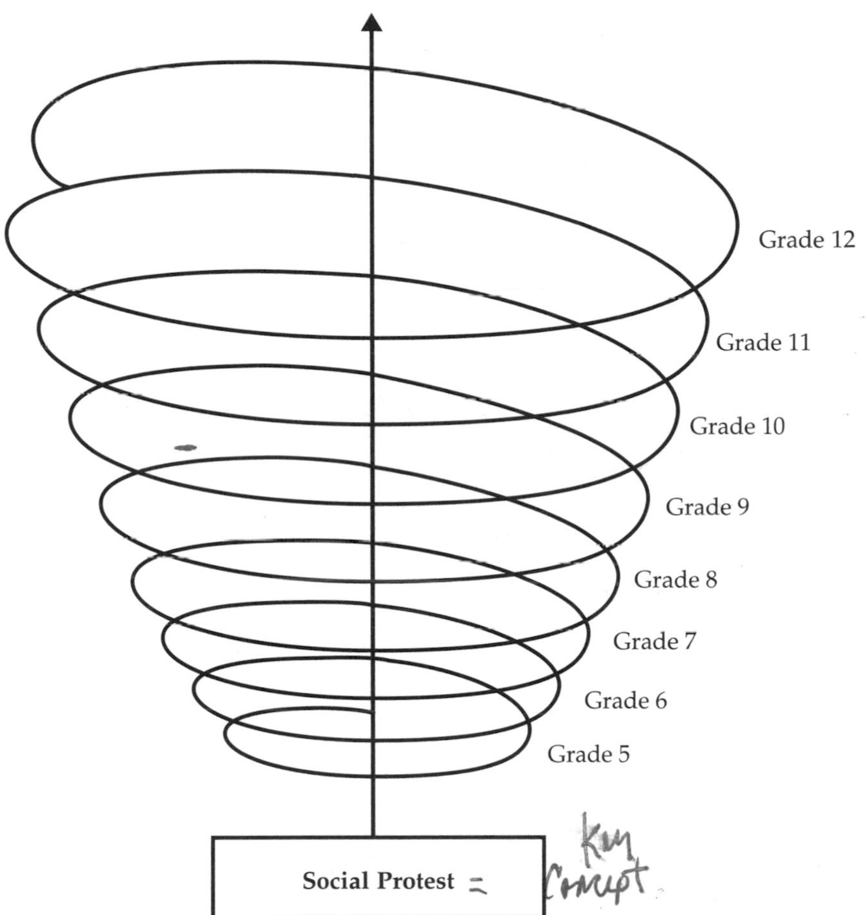

FIGURE 6.1 Social Protest Is Taught at Grades 5 through 12 at an Increasing Degree of Depth and Complexity

ing generalizations and conclusions. The steps of social science inquiry are illustrated in Figure 6.2 on page 73.

Although knowledge and skills goals are very important, it is essential that a multicultural curriculum help students develop the skills needed to reflect on their moral choices and to make thoughtful decisions. I have developed a value inquiry model (described on page 78) that can be used to help students develop value inquiry skills. Students should be provided with opportunities to develop democratic values and to act on their moral decisions. Values education is especially important in multicultural education because prejudice and discrimination, which multicultural education tries to reduce, are heavily value laden. The moral dimension of multicultural education is discussed in the last part of this chapter.

Examples of Lessons Organized with Powerful Concepts

Teaching about Historical Bias and Knowledge Construction

The knowledge construction component of multicultural education helps students understand how knowledge is constructed and how it is influential by the biases, experiences, and perceptions of historians and other researchers (Banks, 1993a; Code, 1991; Collins, 2000; Harding, 1991). It also helps students to construct their own versions of the past, present, and future. In knowledge construction lessons and units, students are active participants in building knowledge rather than passive consumers of the knowledge constructed by others. What follows is a unit written by the author (Banks with Sebesta, 1982) that is designed to teach junior high students how knowledge is constructed in history and about how historical interpretations are derived.

Columbus and the Arawaks

During the fifteenth century, Europeans wanted to find an easy way to reach Asia. They wanted to trade with Asian merchants. Many Europeans knew that the world is round. They believed they could reach Asia by sailing west. Christopher Columbus, an Italian sailor and explorer, was one person who wanted to prove that it could be done. For many years, he tried to find money to sail west to reach Asia, also called the East Indies. Finally, King Ferdinand and Queen Isabella of Spain agreed to support his voyage. On August 3, 1492, Columbus sailed from Palos, Spain. His three small ships were called the Pinta, the Nina, and the Santa Maria. On October 12, 1492, Columbus and his crew landed on San Salvador in the Bahama Islands. The Bahama Islands are located in what are now called the West Indies. We use that name because of the mistake Columbus made. He was sure he had landed near India. Even after other European explorers visited America, people still believed that America was part of the East Indies. This is why the Europeans called the Native Americans "Indians."

Columbus Writes about the Arawaks

In a letter that Columbus wrote in 1493, he tells of meeting with the people he called Indians (Muzzey, 1915, p. 8).

> They believed very firmly that I, with these ships and crews, came from the sky.... Wherever I arrived they went running from house to house and to the

neighboring villages, with loud cries of "Come! Come to see the people from Heaven!"

Columbus Describes the Arawaks at San Salvador

Columbus kept a diary of his first voyage across the ocean. Here is what he wrote about the Arawaks when he first met them on San Salvador (Jane, 1989, pp. 23–24). Does he report facts only? Does he mix his own opinion with the facts?

> In fact, they took all and gave all, such as they had, with good will, but it seemed to me that they were a people very deficient in everything. They all go naked as their mothers bore them, and the women also, although I saw only one very young girl. And all those whom I did see were youths, so that I did not see one who was over thirty years of age; they were very well built, with very handsome bodies and very good faces. Their hair is coarse almost like the hairs of a horse's tail and short; they wear their hair down over their eyebrows, except for a few strands behind, which they wear long and never cut. Some of them are painted black, and they are the colour of the people of the Canaries, neither black nor white, and some of them are painted white and some red and some in any colour that they find. Some of them paint their faces, some their whole bodies, some only the eyes, and some only the nose. They do not bear arms or know them, for I showed to them swords and they took them by the blade and cut themselves through ignorance.
>
> They should be good servants and of quick intelligence, since I see that they very soon say all that is said to them, and I believe that they would easily be made Christians, for it appeared to me that they had no creed. Our Lord willing, at the time of my departure I will bring back six of them to Your Highnesses, that they may learn to talk. I saw no beast of any kind in this island, except parrots.

The Second Voyage of Columbus

Columbus sailed back to Spain on January 16, 1493. Later that same year, he set off on his second voyage. This time he explored other islands, including those now called Puerto Rico, the Virgin Islands, and Jamaica.

On his first trip, Columbus had established a trading post on the island of Hispaniola, where Haiti and the Dominican Republic are now located. When he returned to Hispaniola, he found that his trading post had been destroyed. This is what had happened. The men Columbus had left in charge of the trading post had been cruel to the Arawaks. The Arawaks became angry. One of them was a man named Caonabo (ka o na' bo). He led a group of Arawaks who killed the Spaniards and then destroyed the trading post. When Columbus discovered what had happened, he and his men attacked the Arawaks and defeated them. Caonabo was sent to Spain for punishment.

Columbus's Demands for Gold

Columbus set up a new trading post right away. It was very important for him to find gold in America and send it back to Spain. He had to please the Spanish king and queen.

Columbus did not really have any way of knowing how much gold there was in Hispaniola. In order to get as much gold as possible, he devised a plan. He told the Arawaks in the region yielding the gold that they must honor the Spanish king. Every three months, all of the Arawaks fourteen years old or older had to give Columbus a small amount of gold dust. Each Arawak who gave the gold wore a piece of brass or copper around his or her neck to prove that the payment had been made. Any Arawak found without the neck ornament was punished. There was not enough gold in Hispaniola to satisfy Columbus. The Arawaks could not meet his demand for gold. Some tried to escape to the mountains. Some became ill and died. Some starved. Some who could not pay the gold were tortured and killed. Others were forced to work the land or were sent in slavery to Spain.

Ferdinand, Son of Columbus

Columbus had a son named Ferdinand who went with him on his fourth trip to America in 1502. At that time, Ferdinand was just thirteen years old. When he was grown, Ferdinand wrote about his father in a book called *The Life of the Admiral Christopher Columbus*. Here is what Ferdinand said about the way his father treated the Arawaks (Keen, 1959):

> After the capture of Caonabo the island was so peaceful that a Christian could safely go wherever he pleased, and the Indians themselves offered to carry him piggyback, as they do nowadays at the post stages. Columbus credits this peace to the favor of God and the good fortune of the Catholic monarchs [kings], else it would have been impossible for 200 poorly armed men, half of them sick, to defeat a mass of Indians. But the Lord wished to punish the Indians, and so brought them a shortage of food and such a variety of diseases that he reduced their number by two-thirds, that it might be clear that such wonderful conquests came from His supreme hand and not from our strength or wit or the cowardice of the Indians. (p. 150)

The Arawaks

What was life really like for the Arawaks that Ferdinand believed were "punished" by God? Their culture came to an end a century after the Spaniards came to their home in the Caribbean Islands. But archaeologists, using artifacts, are able to piece together the story of the Arawaks.

An archaeologist named Fred Olsen (1974) studied Arawak artifacts. From what he learned from these artifacts, he wrote a description of what an Arawak community was probably like. He tried to tell what life was like for the Arawaks in 1490, which was two years before Columbus came to San Salvador in the Bahama Islands. Here is Fred Olsen's description of what might have happened during one day in an Arawak village:

> Along the edge of the river men are mending fishing nets. Others are collecting a shrub which contains a fish poison. One man is pounding the roots and stems until they are in shreds like hemp. Some of this mass is thrown into a large pool near the shore of the river. In a matter of minutes fish begin to rise and float on the surface. Young boys wade in, gleefully picking up the fish and bringing them ashore.
>
> At the end of the village pottery is being made by the women. At one spot a brush heap is slowly burning out and the pots lying on the embers are almost fully fired. A few more branches are put on the fire to finish baking the pots.
>
> Nearby two women are kneading the reddish plastic mass they have brought from the valley where good potter's clay is found not far from the river. Small amounts of water and sand are being added until the clay has the desired consistency. Experienced hands roll long rods of clay, about the thickness of a finger, which they coil layer by layer until the basic pot shape is formed. Smooth disks of stone, which they have picked up on the beach, are held snugly in the palm of the hand and the coils rubbed down until the ridges disappear and the bowl takes on a satinlike surface on both the outside and inside walls. (p. 218)

When Columbus first came to the Caribbean Islands in 1492, there were about three hundred thousand Arawaks living there. One hundred years later, almost none remained. Forced labor and diseases destroyed most of the Arawaks.

The Last Journeys of Columbus

Columbus made his two final journeys in 1498 and 1502. During these voyages, he sailed along the coast of Central America and South America. Columbus died in 1506, still thinking he had reached the Indies. He never knew that he had explored the continent of America.

In this unit, you have read about the landing of Columbus in America, and the effect he and other Spaniards had on the Arawaks. In the next chapter, you will read about other European explorers who came to America.

What Do You Think?

1. Columbus wrote in his diary that he thought the Indians had no religious beliefs. You read about Arawak life in the report by Fred Olsen. Do you think Columbus was correct? Why?

2. Accounts written by people who took part in or witnessed (saw) an historical event are called *primary sources*. Can historians believe everything they read in a primary source? Explain.

Things to Do

1. Be an Arawak in 1492. Working with three other classmates, write a response to Columbus's account on page 69.
2. Working in a group with three other students, and using the documents in this unit as your source, write your own account of the Columbus-Arawak encounter. Then answer these questions:
   a. In what ways is your account limited?
   b. What can you do that would make your account less limited?
   c. Are historical accounts always limited no matter how many documents, artifacts, and resources the historian has? Why or why not?
   d. What conclusions can you make about the writing of historical accounts based on this activity?
3. Carl Becker, the famous historian, said that every person was his or her own historian. What did he mean? To what extent is his statement accurate?

Teaching about Revolutions Using Social Science Inquiry

Social Science Inquiry

In the unit on revolutions described below, Ms. Garcia, a senior high school social studies teacher, uses the inquiry model developed by Banks (Banks & Banks, 1999) and illustrated in Figure 6.2 to teach a powerful concept: *revolution*. She uses three American revolutions as content samples: (1) the Pueblo Revolution in 1680, in which the Pueblo tribes of New Mexico revolted against the Spanish; (2) the revolution in the British Colonies (1776); and (3) the Mexican Revolution of 1810

Creating Doubt and Concern: Motivating the Students

Ms. Garcia starts the unit by having the class play the simulation game, *Starpower* (Shirts, 1969). In this game, after a round of trading chips, the players are divided into three groups according to the number of points they have: the squares (with the most points), the circles (with the least points), and the triangles (those in between). Ms. Garcia then distributes the chips in such a way that, without the players knowing it, will keep the squares ahead of the other two groups.

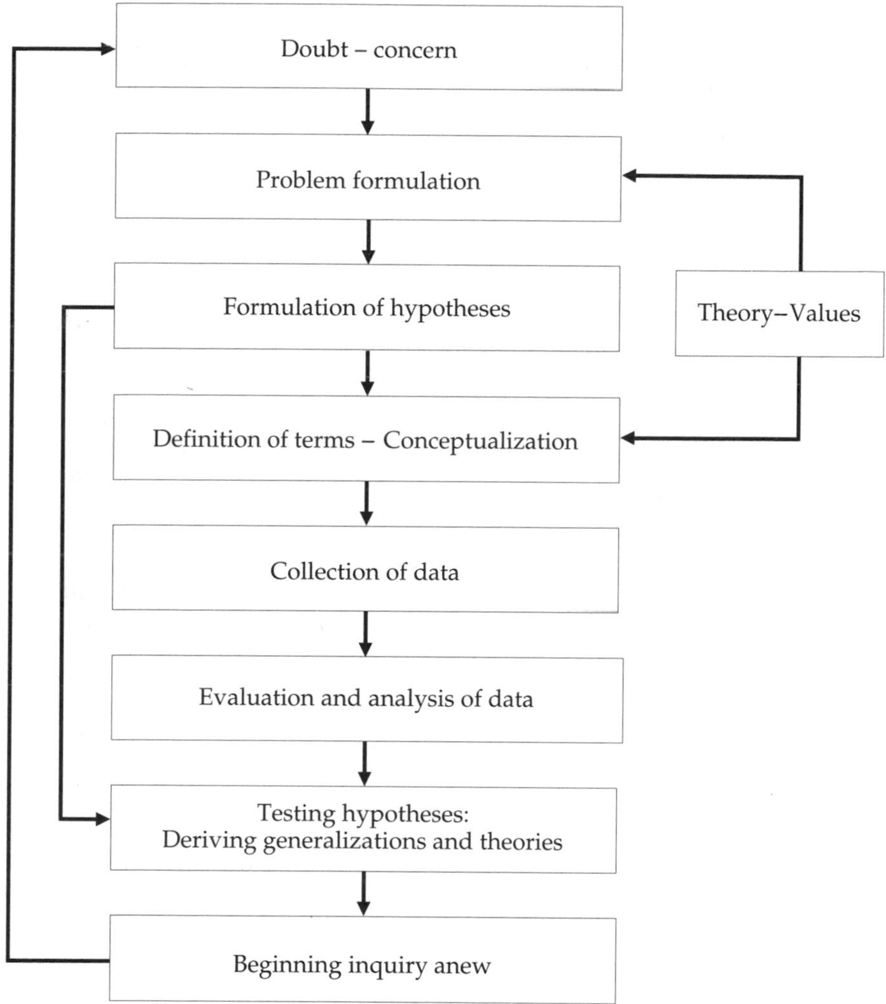

A model of social inquiry. Note that in the inquiry model, doubt and concern cause the inquirer to formulate a problem. The problem that he or she formulates does not emanate from a vacuum, but is shaped by his or her theoretical and value orientation. Like the social scientist, the student will need to draw on *knowledge* to be able to ask intelligent and fruitful questions. In social science inquiry, *theory* is the main source of fruitful questions. While these are the basic steps of social inquiry, they do not necessarily occur in the order illustrated above. This figure indicates that generalizations in social science are continually tested and are never regarded as absolute. Thus, social inquiry is cyclic rather than linear and fixed.

FIGURE 6.2 A Model of Social Inquiry

Source: Reprinted with permission from James A. Banks & Cherry A. McGee Banks (with Ambrose A. Clegg, Jr.) (1999). *Teaching strategies for the social studies: Decision-Making and Citizen Action* (5th ed.). New York: Longman, p. 68.

A highly stratified society is created with little opportunity for mobility. When they are in a clearly dominant position, Ms. Garcia gives the squares the power to make the rules of the game. They make rules that help to keep themselves in power. The circles and the triangles become very angry and frustrated and call the rules dictatorial and fascist. The frustrations become so high that the game ends in a revolt against the rules and the squares.

Formulating Questions and Hypotheses

Ms. Garcia uses the simulation game as a vehicle to start the unit on revolutions and to get the students to formulate questions related to the rise of prerevolutionary conditions in a society. She asks the students:

1. Why did the circles and the triangles become so angry and frustrated?
2. Have you ever had a real-life experience in which you felt this way? If so, what was it? Why did you feel that way? What did you do about it?
3. How did the simulation game end? Why did it end that way?
4. Can you think of examples of people and groups in history and in modern times who felt the way the triangles and circles felt at the end of the game?

Through questions and cues, Ms. Garcia gets the students to discuss these examples: (1) the Pilgrims in seventeenth-century England, who were opposed to the Church of England; (2) the American colonists in the late 1700s, who were angry with Britain about taxation without representation; (3) the Cherokee Indians in the Southeast in the 1830s, who were forced to move from their homeland to Oklahoma; (4) the Jews in Germany in the 1930s and 1940s, who experienced discrimination and persecution; and (5) African Americans in the South during the 1950s and 1960s, who experienced discrimination.

What kinds of conditions made these groups angry? (Ms. Garcia is trying to get the students to state *hypotheses* about conditions that can lead to anger and rebellion. The class keeps a list of its statements about the kinds of conditions that made these groups so angry.)

Ms. Garcia asks the students to list some things that individuals and groups might be able to do when they feel like the triangles and the circles, as did the Jews in Germany in the 1930s and 1940s, or the American colonists in 1776. The students state that these groups might (1) let the authorities know how unhappy they are; (2) try to change the laws and rules; or (3) migrate to another place or nation.

Ms. Garcia then asks: What if none of these things is possible? What if none of them helps to improve the conditions of those who feel mistreated? Then what might they do? Through continual questioning, cues, and examples, Ms. Garcia helps the students to state that if all efforts fail to improve their conditions, then groups might try to overthrow the government, if certain conditions prevail.

Ms. Garcia tells the class that, depending on many conditions within a society, a group that feels mistreated may do many different things, including start a protest movement, migrate, start riots, and, in particular cases, try to overthrow the government. She points out that in most of the examples the class discussed, the groups did not try to overthrow the government. She asks: What particular conditions do you think must exist before a group that is very angry tries to overthrow the government? (Ms. Garcia is trying to get the students to hypothesize about the causes of revolutions. The class keeps a list of the hypotheses it states.)

Ms. Garcia asks the students to give their ideas about what they think happens when the old government is overthrown and a new government is established. (She is trying to get them to state hypotheses about what happens when a revolution occurs and a new government is established.) The class keeps a record of its hypotheses.

Ms. Garcia helps the students to summarize the major questions they have raised and will study during the unit:

1. What kinds of things make groups very angry within a nation or society?
2. What kinds of things do groups do when they are very angry about the way in which the government and officials of a nation are treating them?
3. Under what conditions will groups try to overthrow the government when they feel angry and mistreated?
4. What happens when the government is overthrown?
5. Does the new government remove the conditions that cause the old government to be overthrown?

Defining Concepts

Ms. Garcia tells the class that it has discussed two major ideas that social scientists use specific concepts to describe. The powerlessness and frustration that the triangles and circles felt at the end of the simulation is called *alienation* by sociologists. Alienated individuals and groups feel that they cannot control their destiny or have any significant influence on the important events within their society (Marshall, 1994). She tells the students that when the government of a nation is suddenly overthrown and a new government is established, a *revolution* has taken place. She gives the students Crane Brinton's (1962) definition of a revolution: "The drastic, sudden substitution of one group in charge of the running of a territorial political entity for another group" (p. 4).

Ms. Garcia tells the class that the word *revolution* is used in many different ways (she gives examples of it, meaning a complete change in something) but that it will be used to mean the sudden replacement of one government by another in this unit.

Collecting Data

Ms. Garcia decides to use a combination of lectures, class discussions, and small groups to present and gather data. Drawing on materials primarily from the French Revolution of 1789, Ms. Garcia presents several lectures in which she sketches some of the major reasons that revolutions develop, some of their major characteristics, and what often happens in the postrevolutionary period. Each of her lectures is followed by a discussion session in which she asks the students higher-level questions that help them to develop concepts and generalizations about the characteristics of a revolution and the conditions under which they occur.

Ms. Garcia divides the class into three groups to do independent research on three American revolutions: the *Pueblo Revolution in 1680;* the *Revolution in the English Colonies in 1776;* and the *Mexican Revolution in 1810.* The class develops the data retrieval chart in Table 6.3 to guide the research of each group.

Ms. Garcia also plans some total-class data-gathering activities in addition to her lectures. The students read Chapters 1, 2, and 9 in *The Anatomy of Revolution* by Crane Brinton (1962). In this book, Brinton derives generalizations about revolutions by analyzing four: the English (1649), the American (1776), the French (1789), and the Russian (1917). The students also read George Orwell's (1946) *Animal Farm,* a disguised political satire of the Russian revolution.

Evaluating Data and Deriving Generalizations

When the three research groups collect their data, they analyze the results, making sure that they answer all of the questions in Table 6.3. Each of the three groups presents its findings to the class in a different format. The group that studies the Pueblo Revolution presents its findings to the class in the form of a dramatization. A narrator describes the highlights of the revolution as the other students in the group act them out. This group describes how the Pueblo Revolution ultimately failed when the Pueblos were reconquered by the Spanish:

> Pope was dead. The Pueblo tribes had tired of fighting. They were ill and hungry. Vargas brought an army of less than a hundred soldiers to Santa Fe

> in 1692. Tall, sure of himself and quiet in his manner, he took the town without fighting. Then he went from pueblo to pueblo convincing the Indians once again to accept Spanish rule, never firing a shot. In this way he "conquered" 73 Pueblos for the Spanish.

The English Colonies group prepares a striking mural that depicts the major events in that revolution. The students share this mural when making their class presentation. The Mexican Revolution group presents its findings to the class in a panel discussion.

During and after each group's presentation, using the data retrieval chart in Table 6.3, the class formulates generalizations about the three revolutions. The class discusses ways in which the three revolutions were alike and different. The Pueblo Revolution was the most different from

TABLE 6.3 Data Retrieval Chart on Revolutions

Questions	Pueblo Revolution 1680	Revolution in the English Colonies 1776	Mexican Revolution 1810
Who were the people or groups in power?			
What people or groups wanted power?			
What were the major causes of the revolution?			
What incident(s) triggered the revolution?			
What was gained or lost and by whom?			
What happened immediately afterward?			
What happened in the long run?			

the other two in that it ultimately failed because the Pueblo tribes were eventually reconquered by the Spaniards. The students compare the generalizations they developed with those stated by Brinton in the last chapter of *The Anatomy of Revolution.* They also compare their findings with the view of a revolution presented in Orwell's *Animal Farm* and discuss the extent to which fiction can provide insights into social reality.

When the unit ends, Ms. Garcia not only has succeeded in helping the students to derive concepts and generalizations about revolutions but she also has helped them gain a keen appreciation for the difficulties historians face in reconstructing historical events, establishing cause and effect, and formulating accurate generalizations.

Value Inquiry in the Multicultural Curriculum

The multicultural curriculum should help students to identify, examine, and clarify their values, consider value alternatives, and make reflective value choices they can defend within a society in which human dignity is a shared value. You can use the value inquiry model I developed to help your students to identify and clarify their values and to make reflective moral choices (Banks & Banks, 1999). The Banks value inquiry model consists of these nine steps:

1. Defining and recognizing value problems
2. Describing value-relevant behavior
3. Naming values exemplified by the behavior
4. Determining conflicting values in behavior described
5. Hypothesizing about the possible consequences of the values analyzed
6. Naming alternative values to those exemplified by behavior observed
7. Hypothesizing about the possible consequences of values analyzed
8. Declaring value preferences: choosing
9. Stating reasons, sources, and possible consequences of value choice: justifying, hypothesizing, predicting

You can use a variety of materials and resources to simulate value inquiry and discussion of multicultural issues and topics, such as documents similar to the ones used in the preceding historical inquiry lesson, newspaper feature stories, textbook descriptions of issues and events, and open-ended stories such as the one below. When using the open-ended story below, "Trying to Buy a Home in Lakewood Island" (Banks, 1997b), you can use the value inquiry model to develop questions like the ones that follow the story to simulate value discussion and decision making.

Trying to Buy a Home in Lakewood Island

About a year ago, Joan and Henry Green, a young African American couple, moved from the West Coast to a large city in the Midwest. They moved because Henry finished his Ph.D. in chemistry and took a job at a big university in Midwestern City. Since they have been in Midwestern City, the Greens have rented an apartment in the central area of the city. However, they have decided that they want to buy a house. Their apartment has become too small for the many books and other things they have accumulated during the year. In addition to wanting more space, they also want a house so that they can receive breaks on their income tax, which they do not receive living in an apartment. The Greens also think that a house will be a good financial investment.

The Greens have decided to move into a suburban community. They want a new house and most of the houses within the city limits are rather old. They also feel that they can obtain a larger house for their money in the suburbs than in the city. They have looked at several suburban communities and have decided that they like Lakewood Island better than any of the others. Lakewood Island is a predominantly White community, which is comprised primarily of lower-middle class and middle-class residents. There are a few wealthy families in Lakewood Island. But they are the exceptions rather than the rule.

Joan and Henry Green have become frustrated because of the problems they have experienced trying to buy a home in Lakewood Island. Before they go out to look at a house, they carefully study the newspaper ads. When they arrived at the first house in which they were interested, the owner told them that his house had just been sold. A week later they decided to work with a realtor. When they tried to close the deal on the next house they wanted, the realtor told them that the owner had raised the price $40,000 because he had the house appraised since he had put it on the market and had discovered that his selling price was much too low. When the Greens tried to buy a third house in Lakewood Island, the owner told them that he had decided not to sell because he had not received the job in another city that he was almost sure that he would receive when he had put his house up for sale. He explained that the realtor had not removed the ad about his house from the newspaper even though he had told him that he had decided not to sell a week earlier. The realtor the owner had been working with had left the real estate company a few days ago. Henry is bitter and feels that he and his wife are victims of racial discrimination. Joan believes that Henry is paranoid and that they have been the victims of a series of events that could have happened to anyone, regardless of their race. (pp. 234, 236)

1. What is the main problem in the case?
2. What are the values of Joan Green? Henry Green? The realtor? The owners? What behaviors show the values you have listed?

(continued)

Trying to Buy a Home in Lakewood Island *Continued*

3. How are the values of these individuals alike and different? Why? Joan Green, Henry Green, the realtor, the owners.
4. Why are the values of these individuals alike and different? Joan Green, Henry Green, the realtor, the owners.
5. What are other values that these individuals could embrace? Joan Green, Henry Green, the realtor, the owners.
6. What are the possible consequences of the values and actions of each of these individuals? Joan Green, Henry Green, the realtor, the owners.
7. What should the Greens do?
8. Why should the Greens take this action? What are the possible consequences of the actions you stated above?
9. What would you do if you were the Greens? Why?

Conceptual Teaching and Curriculum Transformation

An important goal of multicultural education is to transform the curriculum so that students develop an understanding of how knowledge is constructed and the extent to which it is influenced by the personal, social, cultural, and gender experiences of knowledge producers (Code, 1991; Collins, 1990; Harding, 1991). Organizing the curriculum around powerful ideas and concepts facilitates the development of teaching strategies and learning experiences that focus on knowledge construction and the development of thinking skills. This chapter has described ways in which a conceptual and transformative multicultural curriculum can be designed and implemented.

CHAPTER

7 Citizenship Education and Teacher Knowledge

Because of the increasing racial, ethnic, cultural, and language diversity in the United States, effective teachers in the new century must help students become reflective citizens in pluralistic democratic nation-states. In this chapter, I argue that citizenship education needs to be reconceptualized because of the increased salience of diversity issues throughout the world. A new kind of citizenship education, called multicultural citizenship, will enable students to acquire a delicate balance of *cultural, national,* and *global* identifications and to understand the ways in which knowledge is constructed; to become knowledge producers; and to participate in civic action to create a more humane nation and world (Banks, 1997a). Teachers must develop reflective cultural, national, and global identifications themselves if they are to help students become thoughtful, caring, and reflective citizens in a multicultural world society.

This chapter consists of two major parts. In the first, I describe the theoretical and conceptual goals for citizenship education in a pluralistic democratic society. In the second, I describe how I implement these goals in one of my teacher education courses.

Balancing Diversity and Unity

Most nation-states and societies throughout the world are characterized by cultural, ethnic, language, and religious diversity. One of the challenges to pluralistic democratic nation-states is to provide opportunities for cultural and ethnic groups to maintain components of their community cultures while at the same time constructing a nation-state in which diverse groups are structurally included and to which they feel allegiance. A delicate balance of unity and diversity should be an essential goal of democratic nation-states.

The challenge of balancing diversity and unity is intensifying as democratic nation-states such as the United States, Canada, Australia, and the

United Kingdom become more diversified and as racial and ethnic groups within these nations become involved in cultural and ethnic revitalization movements. The democratic ideologies institutionalized within the major democratic Western nations and the wide gap between these ideals and realities were major factors that resulted in the rise of ethnic revitalization movements in nation-states such as the United States, Canada, and the United Kingdom during the 1960s and 1970s.

These nations share a democratic ideal, a major tenet of which is that the state should protect human rights and promote equality and the structural inclusion of diverse groups into the fabric of society. These societies are also characterized by widespread inequality and by racial, ethnic, and class stratification. The discrepancy between democratic ideals and societal realities and the rising expectations of structurally excluded racial-, ethnic-, and social-class groups created protest and revival movements within the Western democratic nations.

The Need for a New Conception of Citizenship Education

Because of growing ethnic, cultural, racial, and religious diversity throughout the world, citizenship education needs to be changed in substantial ways to prepare students to function effectively in the twenty-first century. Today's citizens need the knowledge, attitudes, and skills required to function in their ethnic and cultural communities and beyond their cultural borders and to participate in the construction of a national civic culture that is a moral and just community that embodies democratic ideals and values, such as those embodied in the Universal Declaration of Human Rights. Students also need to acquire the knowledge and skills needed to become effective citizens in the global community.

Citizenship education in the past, in the United States as well as in many other nations, embraced an assimilationist ideology. In the United States, its aim was to educate students so they would fit into a mythical Anglo-Saxon Protestant conception of the "good citizen." Anglo conformity was the goal of citizenship education. One of its aims was to eradicate the community cultures and languages of students from diverse ethnic, cultural, racial, and language groups. One consequence of this assimilationist conception of citizenship education was that many students lost their first cultures, languages, and ethnic identities. Some students also became alienated from family and community. Another consequence was that many students became socially and politically alienated within the national civic culture.

Ethnic minorities of color often became marginalized in both their community cultures and in the national civic culture because they could function effectively in neither. When they acquired the language and culture of the Anglo mainstream, they were denied structural inclusion and full participation into the civic culture because of their racial characteristics.

Citizenship education must be transformed because of the large influx of immigrants who are now settling in nations throughout the world, because of the continuing existence of institutional racism and discrimination throughout the world, and because of the widening gap between the rich and the poor.

The U.S. Census (U.S. Census Bureau, 1998) projects that 47 percent of the U.S. population will consist of ethnic minorities of color by 2050. The percentage of ethnic minorities in nation-states throughout the world has increased significantly within the past 30 years. In many Western nations, the ethnic minority population is growing at significantly greater rates than is the majority population. Institutionalized discrimination and racism are manifest by the significant gaps in the incomes, education, and health of minority and majority groups in many nation-states. Ethnic, racial, and religious minorities are also the victims of violence in many nation-states.

In the United States, the share of the nation's wealth held by the wealthiest households (0.5%) rose sharply in the 1980s after declining for 40 years. In 1976, this segment of the population held 14 percent of the nation's wealth. In 1983, it held 26.9 percent (Phillips, 1990). In 1997, 12.7 percent of Americans, which included a higher percentage of African Americans and Hispanics (8.6% of non-Hispanic Whites, 26.0% of African Americans, 27.1% of Hispanics), were living in poverty (U.S. Census Bureau, 1998).

Cultural Communities and Multicultural Citizenship

Citizens should be able to maintain attachments to their cultural communities as well as participate effectively in the shared national culture. Cultural and ethnic communities need to be respected and given legitimacy not only because they provide safe spaces for ethnic, cultural, and language groups on the margins of society, but also because they serve as a conscience for the nation-state. These communities take action to force the nation to live up to its democratic ideals when they are most seriously violated. It was the abolitionists and not the founding fathers in the United States who argued that freedom and equality should be extended to all Americans. African Americans led the civil rights movement of the 1960s and 1970s that forced the United States to eradicate its system of racial apartheid.

Okihiro (1994) points out that people and groups in the margins have been the conscience of the United States throughout its history. They have kept the United States committed to its democratic ideals as stated in its founding documents: the Declaration of Independence, the

Constitution, and the Bill of Rights. He argues that the margins have been the main sites for keeping democracy and freedom alive in the United States. It was the groups in the margins that reminded and forced America to live up to its democratic ideals when they were most severely tested. Examples include (a) slavery and the middle passage, (b) Indian removal in the 1830s, (c) the internment of Japanese Americans during World War II, and (d) segregation and apartheid in the South that crumbled during the 1960s and 1970s in response to the African American-led civil rights movement. In *The Story of American Freedom,* Foner (1998) makes an argument similar to Okihiro's:

> The authors of the notion of freedom as a universal birthright, a truly human ideal, were not so much the founding fathers who created a nation dedicated to liberty but resting in large measure on slavery, but abolitionists...and women. (p. xx)

A new kind of citizenship is needed for the twenty-first century, which Kymlicka (1995) calls "multicultural citizenship." It recognizes and legitimizes the right and need of citizens to maintain commitments both to their ethnic and cultural communities and to the national civic culture. Only when the national civic culture is transformed in ways that reflect and give voice to the diverse ethnic, racial, language, and religious communities that constitute it will it be viewed as legitimate by all of its citizens. Only then can they develop clarified commitments to the commonwealth and its ideals.

The Assimilationist Fallacy and Citizenship Education

An assimilationist conception of citizenship will not be effective in today's multicultural world because it is based on a serious fallacy. The assimilationist assumes that the most effective way to reduce strong ethnic boundaries, attachments, and affiliations within a nation-state is to provide marginalized and excluded ethnic and racial groups opportunities to experience equality in the nation's social, economic, and political institutions. As they begin to participate more fully in the mainstream society and institutions, argues the assimilationist, marginalized cultural and ethnic groups will focus less on their specific concerns and more on national issues and priorities (Patterson, 1977).

When ethnic groups experience equality, argues the assimilationist, ethnic attachments die of their own weight. The assimilationist views the ideal society as one in which there are no traces of ethnic or racial attachments. All groups will share one dominant national and overarching culture; people will forsake their ethnic cultures when they are structurally included in the national civic culture and community.

Apter (1977) calls the assimilationist position the "assimilationist fallacy." This position holds that as modernization occurs, ethnic groups experience social, political, and economic equality, and commitments to ethnic and community attachments weaken and disappear. Ethnicity, argues the assimilationist, promotes division, exhumes ethnic conflicts, and leads to divisions within society. It also promotes group rights over the rights of the individual.

As Apter (1977) keenly observes, the assimilationist conception is not so much wrong as it is an incomplete and inadequate explanation of ethnic realities in modernized, pluralistic, and democratic nation-states. Ethnicity and assimilationism coexist in modernized democratic nation-states. As Apter suggests, "The two tendencies, toward and against [ethnicity], can go on at the same time. Indeed, the more development and growth that takes place, the more some [ethnic] groupings have to gain by their parochialism" (p. 65).

Ethnicity and modernity coexist in part because of what assimilationists call the "pathological condition"; that is, ethnic groups such as Mexicans in the United States and Afro-Caribbeans in the United Kingdom maintain attachments to their ethnic groups and cultures in part because they have been excluded from full participation in the social, economic, and political institutions of their nation-states.

However, members of marginalized ethnic groups, as well as more privileged ethnic and cultural groups such as Greeks and Jews in the United States, maintain ethnic affiliations and ethnic attachments for more fundamental psychological and sociological reasons. Ethnicity helps them to fulfill some basic psychological and sociological needs that the "thin" culture of modernization leaves starving. Apter (1977) comments insightfully on this point:

> [Ethnic revival] is a response to the thinning out of enlightenment culture, the deterioration of which is a part of the process of democratization and pluralization.... Assimilation itself then vitiates the enlightenment culture. As it does, it leaves what might be called a *primordial space* [italics added], a space people try to fill when they believe they have lost something fundamental and try to recreate it. (p. 75)

Multicultural citizenship education allows students to maintain attachments to their cultural and ethnic communities while at the same time helping them to attain the knowledge and skills needed to participate in the wider civic culture and community.

Helping Students to Develop Cultural, National, and Global Identifications

Citizenship education should help students to develop thoughtful and clarified identifications with their cultural communities and their nation-states. It should also help students to develop clarified global identifications and deep understandings of their roles in the world community

(Diaz, Massialas, & Xanthopoulos, 1999). Students need to understand how life in their cultural communities and nations influences other nations, as well as the cogent effect that international events have on their daily lives. Global education should have as major goals helping students to develop understandings of the interdependence among nations in the world today, clarified attitudes toward other nations, and reflective identifications with the world community.

Developing a Delicate Balance of Identifications

Nonreflective and unexamined cultural attachments may prevent the development of a cohesive nation with clearly defined national goals and policies. Although we need to help students to develop reflective and clarified cultural identifications, they must also be helped to clarify and strengthen their identifications with their nation-states. However, blind nationalism will prevent students from developing reflective and positive global identifications. Nationalism and national attachments in most nations of the world are strong and tenacious. An important aim of citizenship education should be to help students develop global identifications and a deep understanding of the need to take action as citizens of the global community to help solve the world's difficult global problems.

Cultural, national, and global experiences and identifications are interactive and interrelated in a dynamic way. Writes Arnove (1999),

> There is a dialect at work by which...global processes interact with national and local actors and contexts to be modified, and in some cases transformed. There is a process of give-and-take, an exchange by which international trends are reshaped to local ends. (pp. 2–3)

Students should develop a delicate balance of cultural, national, and global identifications (see Figure 7.1). However, educators often try to help students develop strong national identifications by eradicating their ethnic and community cultures and making students ashamed of their families, community beliefs, languages, and behaviors.

I believe that cultural, national, and global identifications are developmental in nature, that individuals can attain healthy and reflective national identifications only when they have acquired healthy and reflective cultural identifications, and that individuals can develop reflective and positive global identifications only after they have realistic, reflective, and positive national identifications (J. A. Banks, 2001). These identifications are dynamic and interactive; they are not discrete.

Individuals can develop a clarified commitment to and identification with a nation-state and the national culture only when they believe that

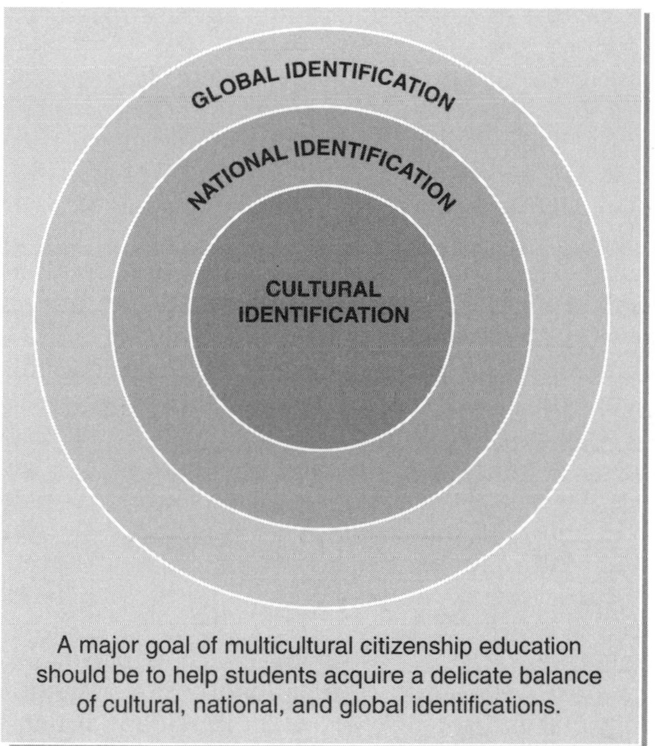
GLOBAL IDENTIFICATION
NATIONAL IDENTIFICATION
CULTURAL IDENTIFICATION
A major goal of multicultural citizenship education should be to help students acquire a delicate balance of cultural, national, and global identifications.

FIGURE 7.1 Cultural, National, and Global Identifications

they are a meaningful part of the nation-state and that it acknowledges, reflects, and values their culture and them as individuals. A nation-state that alienates and does not structurally include all cultural groups into the national culture runs the risk of creating alienation and causing groups to focus on specific concerns and issues rather than on the overarching goals and policies of the nation-state.

Multicultural Citizenship Education, Knowledge, and Action

To help students acquire reflective and clarified cultural, national, and global identifications, citizenship education must teach them *to know, to care, and to act*. As Paulo Freire (1985) points out, students must be taught to read the word and the world. In other words, they must acquire higher levels of knowledge, understand the relationship between knowledge and action, develop a commitment to act to improve the world, and acquire the skills needed to participate in civic action. Multicultural citizens take actions within their communities and nations to make the world more humane. Multicultural citizenship education helps students learn how to act to change the world.

To become thoughtful and effective citizen actors, students must understand the ways in which knowledge is constructed and how knowledge production is related to the location of knowledge producers in the social, political, and economic contexts of society. Multicultural citizenship education must also help students to become knowledge producers themselves and to use the knowledge they have acquired and constructed to take democratic social and civic action.

I have conceptualized five types of knowledge that can help educators to teach about knowledge construction (J. A. Banks, 1996a): (a) personal/cultural knowledge, (b) popular knowledge, (c) mainstream academic knowledge, (d) transformative academic knowledge, and (e) school knowledge. Although the categories of this ideal-type typology can be conceptually distinguished, in reality they overlap and are interrelated in a dynamic way. *Mainstream academic knowledge* and *transformative academic knowledge* are briefly defined below because these concepts are used in the discussion in the second part of this chapter.

Mainstream academic knowledge consists of the concepts, paradigms, theories, and explanations that constitute traditional and established knowledge in the behavioral and social sciences. An important assumption within mainstream knowledge is that objective truths can be verified through rigorous and objective research procedures that are uninfluenced by human interests, values, and perspectives (Homans, 1967).

Transformative academic knowledge consists of the concepts, paradigms, themes, and explanations that challenge mainstream academic knowledge and that expand the historical and literary canon (J. A. Banks, 1996c, 2001; Limerick, 2000). Transformative scholars assume that knowledge is influenced by personal values, the social context, and factors such as race, class, and gender. Whereas the primary goal of mainstream academic knowledge is to build theory and explanations, an important goal of transformative knowledge is to use knowledge to change society to make it more just and humane.

The Knowledge Construction Process and Student Identifications

The knowledge construction process describes the ways in which teachers help students to understand, investigate, and determine how the implicit cultural assumptions, frames of reference, perspectives, and biases within a discipline influence the ways in which knowledge is constructed. When the knowledge construction process is implemented in the classroom, teachers help students to understand how knowledge is created and how it is influenced by the racial, ethnic, social class, and gender positions of individuals and groups.

When students participate in knowledge construction, they challenge the mainstream academic metanarrative and construct liberatory and transformative ways of conceptualizing the U.S. and world experience. Understanding the knowledge construction process and participating in it themselves help students to construct clarified cultural, national, and global identifications and to become knowledgeable, caring, and active citizens in democratic societies.

Implications for Teacher Knowledge

Helping Teachers to Develop Clarified Cultural and National Identifications

Teachers need to develop reflective cultural and national identifications if they are to function effectively in diverse classrooms and help students from different cultures and groups to construct clarified identifications. Several characteristics of U.S. teachers and teacher education students make it difficult and problematic for them to develop reflective cultural and national identifications.

Most of the nation's teacher education students are middle-class White females who have little experience with other racial, ethnic, or social-class groups. Even when they come from working-class backgrounds, teacher education students tend to distance themselves from their class origins and to view themselves as middle class in values, perspectives, and behaviors. This occurs in part because White students who come from lower- and working-class communities and cultures—like students of color—must distance themselves from their community cultures to experience academic and social success in educational institutions. This is true not only in the United States but also in other nations, as is epitomized in this statement by a Canadian Ukrainian who recalls his school experiences (Diakiw, 1994):

> This [school] was not an environment in which I was able to talk proudly about my heritage. I retreated and assimilated as fast as I could. I was ashamed of my background. I was particularly embarrassed about my parents. Compared to my friends' parents, mine seemed ignorant and crude.... I visited in their homes but not until the end of grade thirteen did I invite any friends to mine. Only then did I realize that despite the differences in culture and wealth, my parents were among the best. (p. 54)

When teacher education students from working-class backgrounds distance themselves from their class origins, they become less able to connect their childhood experiences with those of low-income and working-class students of color. Consequently, they are less likely to develop an empathetic understanding of students whose behaviors and values conflict with those of the school's mainstream culture (Erickson, 2001).

One of the consequences of the monocultural experiences and the privileged racial and class status of many White college students in teacher education programs is their tendency to view themselves as noncultural and nonoethnic beings who are colorblind and raceless. Consequently, they often view race and culture as something possessed by outsiders and others and view themselves as "just Americans." These kinds of perceptions and perspectives often lead majority-group students to ask these kinds of question during class discussions: "Why do we have to focus on race and other kinds of differences? Why can't we all be just Americans?"

The culturally isolated experiences of many teacher education students, reinforced by their assimilationist high school education and the popular culture, result in their accepting without question the metanarrative of U.S. history that has dominated the nation's curriculum since the late 1800s. The metanarrative that is institutionalized within the nation's schools, colleges, and universities is called *American exceptionalism* by historians such as Appleby (1992) and Kammen (1997).

The institutionalized metanarrative conceptualizes the development of U.S. history as a linear movement of Europeans from the East to the West Coast of the United States, a movement that was ordained by God to bring civilization to the West, which was a wilderness and a frontier. These words connote that the lands on which the Native Americans lived were uninhabited until the Europeans arrived in the West.

Frederick Jackson Turner (1894/1989), in a paper presented at the 1893 meeting of the American Historical Association that was destined to become a classic, characterized the frontier as "the meeting point between savagery and civilization" (p. 3). Turner's characterization of the West epitomizes the metanarrative that is institutionalized in the nation's schools, colleges, and universities. However, the established metanarrative, which I call "mainstream academic knowledge" (J. A. Banks, 1996a) and Apple (1993) describes as "official knowledge," has been strongly challenged by transformative scholars within the past 30 years (C. A. M. Banks, 1996a; Limerick, 2000). The use of concepts such as *wilderness, frontier,* and *westward movement* are legacies of Turner's frontier thesis and the times in which he lived and worked. Cherry McGee Banks (1996a) describes the serious limitations of the mainstream metanarrative:

> By telling part of the story and leaving other parts of the story out, metanarratives suggest not only that some parts of the story don't count, but that

> some parts don't even exist. The exclusive nature of metanarratives, their canonized place in formal school curricula, and the extent to which they are woven into the societal curriculum result in metanarratives producing a feeling of well-being and comfort within mainstream society and their validity rarely being questioned. (p. 49)

The strong and persistent challenge that transformative scholars of color and women have directed toward mainstream academic knowledge since the mid-1960s has resulted in significant curriculum changes in the nation's schools, colleges, and universities and in textbooks. However, despite these substantial changes, many of the concepts, perspectives, and periodizations of the mainstream metanarrative are still deeply embedded in the curriculum, in textbooks, and in the popular culture.

Helping Teacher Education Students Rethink Race, Culture, and Ethnicity

To develop clarified cultural and national identifications, teacher education students must be helped to critically analyze and rethink their notions of race, culture, and ethnicity and to view themselves as cultural and racial beings. They also need to reconstruct race, culture, and ethnicity in ways that are inclusive and that reveal the ways in which these concepts are related to the social, economic, and political structures in U.S. society (Nieto, 1999; Omi & Winant, 1994).

Teacher education students need to understand, for example, the ways in which the statement, "I am not ethnic; I am just American," reveals the privileged position of an individual who is proclaiming his or her own unique culture as American and other cultures as non-American. A statement such as "I don't see color" reveals a privileged position that refuses to legitimize racial identifications that are very important to people of color and that are often used to justify inaction and perpetuation of the status quo. If educators do not "see" color and the ways in which institutionalized racism privileges some groups and disadvantages others, they will be unable to take action to eliminate racial inequality in schools.

In an important ethnographic study of a school, Schofield (2001) found that teachers who said they were colorblind suspended African American males at highly disproportionate rates and failed to integrate content about African Americans into the curriculum. Colorblindness was used to justify inaction and the perpetuation of institutionalized discrimination within the school. Colorblindness is part of the "racial text" of teacher education which, as Cochran-Smith (2000) points out, teachers and teacher educators must "unlearn."

In the first course I teach for teacher education students, I incorporate readings, activities, lectures, and discussions designed to help students construct new concepts of race, culture, and ethnicity. Most students in the course are White women. These activities are designed, in part, to help the students "unlearn racism" and to read the "racial text" of U.S. society and popular culture (Cochran-Smith, 2000). Assignments include a personal reflection paper on the *book We Can't Teach What We Don't Know: White Teachers, Multiracial Schools* (Howard, 1999) as well as a family history project.

In his book, Howard (1999) describes his personal journey as a White person to come to grips with racial issues and to become an effective educator. He speaks in a personal and engaging way to White teachers. In their reflection papers, my students describe their powerful reactions to Howard's book and how it helps them to rethink their personal journey related to race and their ideas about race. Howard makes racism explicit for most of my students for the first time in their lives.

In their family history project, the students are asked not only to provide a brief account of their family's historical journey but also to give explicit attention to the ways in which race, class, and gender have influenced their family and personal histories. Although the family history project is a popular assignment, most of the students have to struggle to describe ways in which race has influenced their family and personal histories because race is largely invisible to them (McIntosh, 1997). Gender is much more visible to my women students. More of the female than male students are able to relate gender to their family and personal stories in meaningful ways.

Challenging the Metanarrative

A series of activities in the course is designed to help students examine the U.S. metanarrative, to construct new conceptions and narratives that describe the development of U.S. history and culture (which I call transformative knowledge), and to think of creative and effective ways to teach new conceptions of the American experience to students. These activities include historical readings, discussions, and role-playing events about U.S. ethnic and racial groups (Banks, 1997a), with the emphasis on the history of ethnic groups of color. The perspectives in these historical accounts are primarily those of the groups being studied rather than those of outsiders.

The perspectives of both insiders and outsiders are needed to give students a comprehensive understanding of U.S. history and culture. However, I emphasize the perspectives of insiders in this course because my students have been exposed to outsider perspectives for most of their prior education. I also focus on insider perspectives because one of the most important goals of the course is to help students learn how to challenge and critically analyze the mainstream metanarrative they have learned during their high school and college years.

The historical readings in my course are supplemented by videotapes that powerfully depict the perspectives of ethnic groups of color on historical and contemporary events. These videotapes include *The Shadow of Hate: A History of Intolerance in America* (Guggenheim, 1995), which chronicles how various groups within the United States, including the Irish, Jews, and African Americans, have been victimized by discrimination. One of the most trenchant examples of discrimination in the videotape is the description of the way Leo Frank, a Jewish northerner living in Atlanta, became a victim of anti-Semitism and racial hostility when he was accused of murdering a White girl who worked in a pencil factory he co-owned.

The Leo Frank case provides the students an opportunity to understand the ways in which race is a social construction, is contextual, and how the meaning of race has changed historically and continues to change today (Jacobson, 1998). Leo Frank was considered Jewish and not White in 1915 Atlanta. In a lecture, I provide the students an overview of Karen Brodkin's (1998) book that describes the process by which Jews became White in America and what the experiences of Jews and other White ethnics, such as the Irish and Italians, reveal about the characteristics of race in the United States.

Brodkin (1998) argues that Jews had to assimilate mainstream American behaviors, ideologies, attitudes, and perspectives to become White. Among the important attitudes they had to acquire, she argues, were the institutionalized attitudes and perceptions that mainstream Whites held toward groups of color. Brodkin argues, as does Toni Morrison (1992), that Whites defined themselves in opposition to African Americans, and that this oppositional definition was one important way in which disparate groups of White ethnics were able to form a collectivity in the United States and to construct themselves as one cultural and identity group.

Ignatiev (1995) describes the ways in which the Irish, like other White ethnic groups, became White by acquiring mainstream White values and behaviors directed against ethnic groups of color. My students are always surprised to learn how the meaning of race has changed through time and that the idea that Whites are one racial group is a rather recent historical development.

I use a videotape that deals with a contemporary Native American issue to relate historical events to current issues and to help the students understand the ways in which our nation's past and present are connected. *In Whose Honor?* (Rosenstein, 1997) chronicles the struggle of Charlene Teters, a Native American graduate student, to end the use of a Native American chief as a football team mascot at the University of Illinois in Champaign-Urbana. The team is called The Fighting Illini, after Chief Illiniwek. During halftime, a student dresses up as Chief Illiniwek and dances. Teters considers the chief and the dance sacrilegious and demeaning to Native Americans. The videotape describes the social action taken by Teters to end the tradition, as well as the strong opposition by the board of trustees and alumni, who want to maintain a tradition that is deeply beloved by vocal and influential alumni and board members. The people who defend the 70-year-old tradition cannot understand how anyone can find it offensive.

In Whose Honor? (Rosenstein, 1997) helps the students understand how the construction of *Indian* in U.S. society is controlled by mainstream institutions, including the mainstream media. Through questioning and discussion, I help the students relate Columbus's construction of the Native people of the Caribbean as Indians, Cortes's construction of the Aztecs as savages, Turner's construction of the West as a wilderness, and the selection of Chief Illiniwek as a mascot. We discuss the following questions to uncover ways in which these events are connected (Banks, 2000):

1. Which groups have the power to define and institutionalize their conceptions within the schools, colleges, and universities?
2. What is the relationship between knowledge and power? Who exercises the most power in this case study?
3. Who benefits from the ways in which Native Americans have been and are often defined in U.S. society? Who loses?
4. How can views of Native Americans be reconstructed in ways that will help empower Native American groups and create more justice in society?

An Unfinished Journey

My project to help teacher education students develop reflective cultural and national identifications is a work in progress that has rewards, challenges, unrealized possibilities, conflicts, and—at times—frustrations for my students and me. My work on global identifications and issues is incomplete and episodic. Each time I teach the course, I feel that I do not have enough time to deal with cultural and national issues. Global issues remain mostly an unrealized and hoped-for goal (Diaz, Massialas, & Xanthopoulos, 1999). Making links when discussing cultural and national issues is the extent to which I deal with global issues in the course.

The class is an unfinished journey for the students and me in several important ways. It is a beginning of what I hope will be a lifelong journey for them. I realize that one course with a transformative goal can have only a limited influence on the knowledge, beliefs, and values of students who have been exposed to mainstream knowledge and perspectives for most of their prior education. Students are required to take a second multicultural education course in our teacher education program. Also, other members of the teacher education faculty are trying to integrate ethnic, cultural, and racial content into the foundations and methods courses.

My course is also an unfinished journey because I am still trying to figure out how to achieve the delicate balance of showing respect for my students while at the same time encouraging them to seriously challenge their deeply held beliefs, attitudes, values, and knowledge claims. I am also trying to conceptualize effective ways to determine the short-term and long-term effectiveness of the course. The opinions of most of my students when the course ends are encouraging. However, I cannot predict the relationship between these opinions and the behavior of the students when they become teachers.

When I taught the class in fall 1999, 21 of 25 students wrote positive and detailed responses to the following question on the University of Washington's standardized course evaluation form: "Was this class intellectually stimulating? Did it stretch your thinking? Yes No Why or Why not?"

However, I worry about the four students in this class of 25 who merely checked "Yes" in answer to the question and made no further comments. The responses of these four students evoke these questions: What are the meanings of their terse responses? In what ways might these students differ from the others who wrote detailed comments? Do they need a different kind of course and a different set of experiences? How will these four students, as well as the other 21 students, view the experience in my course a year after they have been teaching? Will the course make a difference in the ways in which they teach and deal with multicultural content? I was heartened to read in a study reported by Ladson-Billings (1999) that some of the students in a teacher education program who had been "the most resistant to the program's emphasis on equity and diversity issues feel that it has been most beneficial to them in their teaching" (p. 116).

My observations of my students during this 10-week course, reading of their reflection papers and other papers, listening to their class discussions, having conversations with them, and studying their end-of class course evaluations indicate that most of them attain some of the important course objectives. They develop an understanding of how knowledge is constructed, how it relates to power, and how the mainstream metanarrative privileges some groups and marginalizes others. They also develop a better understanding of race, culture, and ethnicity and begin the process of questioning some of their assumptions about these concepts. Perhaps most important, most of my students begin to view their own cultural and racial journeys from different and more critical perspectives. I believe that these critical perspectives will help them to develop more reflective cultural, national, and global identifications.

Teachers with the knowledge and skills I teach in my course are better able to interrogate the assumptions of official school knowledge, less likely to be victimized by knowledge that protects hegemony and inequality, and better able to help students acquire the knowledge and skills needed to take citizen action that will make the world more just and humane.

CHAPTER

8 A Pedagogy for Re-Envisioning America

Margaret Smith Crocco Interviews James A. Banks

Multicultural Education: For Accuracy's Sake

CROCCO: On page 5 of your book, *Multicultural Education, Transformative Knowledge, and Action,* (Banks, 1996c), you write, "Multicultural education is an education for functioning effectively in a pluralistic, democratic society." There are two aspects of this definition I'd like to ask you about. In some of the writing on multicultural education, the stress is on the compensatory role for students of color in terms of self-esteem. That's not something I see emphasized in your definition. Is it implicit in your definition, or is it really less important to you than the conceptualization you give here?

BANKS: First, I'd like to acknowledge that this is a very important question to which I am pleased to have an opportunity to respond. I think there's a great deal of confusion, particularly among the critics of multicultural education, who see it primarily as compensatory, and who challenge its compensatory purpose. The compensatory goal is not the most important one in the way that I conceptualize multicultural education. The main justification for multicultural education is the same as the one for history and geography in the curriculum. Multicultural content helps students to acquire an accurate view of America and an accurate view of the world. Multicultural education is about helping to make our view of America more accurate and more complete because historically it's been incomplete and inaccurate because so many voices and perspectives have been left out.

The most important rationale for multicultural education is to teach students an accurate view of the United States and the world. In order to teach students an accurate view, it is really essential for them to see the westward movement from the points of view of women as well as slavery from the perspectives of people who were enslaved. So often we have taught these events only from the perspectives of men and of slave owners. We need to teach students the perspectives of the Lakota Sioux on the westward movement and the perspectives of Mexicans on the Treaty of Guadalupe Hidalgo.

Multicultural education is for the sake of accuracy. I guess I'm arguing that accuracy is its first and most important goal. A second response to your question: I'd like to suggest that multicultural education, then, is needed as much by the White child in Scarsdale as it is by the African American child in Harlem. It's needed by all of our students because, first, all of our students need accuracy, or as close as we can get to it. The more perspectives we have, the more closely we approximate accuracy. Second, multicultural education is needed by all students—as much by White children in the suburbs as it is by Latino children in inner-city communities.

That leads then to the question of what is the compensatory function of multicultural education. I'd like to deconstruct the established notion of *compensatory* and have us think about it in a new way. I think it's compensatory in the sense that it is helping to make established school history more accurate. In that sense it's compensatory. That's one way of thinking of it as compensatory. Of course, the usual way of thinking of multicultural education as compensatory is thinking of it as doing something to bolster the self-concept of African American and Mexican American students. I think that's the least convincing claim for multicultural education.

Clearly we need to have African American voices in the curriculum; people need to see themselves in the curriculum, but I think the argument ought to be for the sake of democracy, for the sake of giving all students and cultures a voice. The claim that multicultural content will affect student achievement is not an argument I find very convincing. We don't have much evidence to support that claim.

Multicultural Education and National Survival

CROCCO: I'd like to note here the work that Emily Style has done in *Transformations,* a journal published by the New Jersey Project on multiculturalism. Style talks about the "diversity literacy" necessary for the United States in the next century. It's important for all of our students to recognize the multiplicity of voices and experiences in the democratic project, isn't it?

BANKS: I resonate to this question, your notion of diversity literacy because I called a similar concept "multicultural literacy" in one of my articles (Banks, 1991b). I made a similar argument that multicultural literacy was needed to function effectively not only within and across borders in the United States, but also in the world. Our world is shrinking. I am reminded of an anecdote that comes from Mexico. In this particular town, the Mexican inhabitants of that community indicated that they purchased more Japanese cars than American cars, and they were asked why. They said that when the Japanese came to their town they spoke Spanish.

I think that this is indicative of the necessity, if we are to be economically successful, if we are to be effective in the global order, for all of our students to learn to function not only within their own ethnic communities, but also beyond their communities and the United States, and also to function effectively on the global stage. I think that's really important if we are to maintain our leadership role in the twenty-first century. So I think multicultural literacy is needed, not only for the sake of harmony, but also for the sake of our survival.

Ideological Impediments, Resistance, and National Activity in Multicultural Education

CROCCO: In your view today, what's the biggest impediment to bringing the multicultural education vision into general practice in our nation's schools? I'm wondering whether there are national initiatives occurring. In New Jersey and New York, for example, there are many efforts in this regard. Also, could you comment on the effect of national standards on this process, and on the backlash against multiculturalism that's occurring in the popular press? In works like Richard Bernstein's *Dictatorship of Virtue* (1994), there does seem to be a strong attack on multicultural ideas.

BANKS: Let me start with the first question, but give an answer to the last part of it. You asked what the biggest impediment is. The biggest impediment is ideological. I think there is an ideological struggle going on; one might even say an ideological war between several conceptions. One view is held by people who are holding onto a notion of America as they believe it once was, and I stress the word *believe.* I'm thinking of what may be called the Western traditionalists, who are struggling to hold onto an America as they remember it, an America that they believe existed. I have serious doubts as to whether their remembered America ever really existed. Some research suggests that maybe Shakespeare was never studied as widely or was as universally loved as they remember (Carnochan, 1993).

The Western traditionalists are arguing that we ought to maintain the canon and that we are a Western nation. In this ideological war there are the Afrocentrists, who are arguing that the curriculum for African American children should be African-centered and that it should, by extension, be Hispanic-centered, and so forth (Asante, 1998). Then there are the people like me who argue for what we call the multicultural vision (Banks, 1997b). There is an ideological war, and I think this war is the biggest impediment to the implementation of multicultural programs. Related to the ideological war is a power struggle. The Western traditionalists clearly have the power in this struggle, at least for the time being. They exercise power in the media. They have the power to dictate curricula despite all the claims about Shakespeare being thrown out. If you look at the research, for example, in a chapter on the college curriculum in the *Handbook of Research on Multicultural Education,* Ann K. Fitzgerald and Paul Lauter (1995) point out that the college and university curriculum is still primarily Western and male.

In this ideological war, the people who still have the most power are the Western traditionalists. However, I'm not sure that their power can be maintained. I think that's part of what the struggle is about. Their power may not be maintained because of the changes in demographics and the push by groups on the margins for inclusion. I think the biggest impediments to the effective implementation of the multicultural project are ideological resistance and power resistance. Both relate to a power struggle. I don't know if you want me to talk more about that before discussing national activity and national standards. Do you want me to talk more about why there is resistance to multicultural education? I stated some of these points in my first Sachs lecture at Teachers College, Columbia University (Banks, 1996b).

CROCCO: Recapitulate a bit of that because it is important for a clear understanding of the struggle as you see it today.

BANKS: I want to talk about a couple of the reasons I think there is a struggle and a debate. One reason there's a struggle is that there is a real racial crisis in the United States. The debate over multiculturalism reflects the racial divide in the United States. I won't go into great detail, but there are many indications of such a racial divide. For example, if we look at the survey data, they indicate that White Americans by and large believe that affirmative action is not needed, whereas most African Americans believe that it is still needed. Whites and African Americans responded very differently to this question asked on a USA/CNN poll (*USA Today,* 1995): Are affirmative action programs still needed to help women and minorities? Eighty-two percent of Blacks said yes, and 16 percent said no. Forty-four percent of Whites answered yes; 52 percent answered no.

So I think part of the struggle reflects a racial divide. Second, I think the debate and the struggle reflect the changing ethnic texture of the nation, with the growing number of immigrants coming from Latin America and Asia. The census projects that by the year 2050 about 47.5 percent of the nation's population will be people of color (U.S. Census Bureau, 1994). This makes the Western traditionalists very afraid and nervous. It's more legitimate to attack multicultural education than to be viewed as an outright nativist or racist.

Attacking multicultural education is a legitimate way to express fear and concerns. Third, I think the debate over multiculturalism reflects the widening gap between the rich and the poor. For example, in 1992 the top 20 percent of U.S. households received 11 times as much income as did the bottom 20 percent. The effect was to give the richest 20 percent of households a 45 percent share of the country's total net income in 1992, which was a postwar high, and the poorest 20 percent of households, a mere 4 percent share. (These data are from an article in the *Economist,* November 5, 1995.)

Finally, I think the debate over multiculturalism reflects the concern by the most powerful groups in U.S. society that they will lose power if they share it, and if women and people of color become structurally integrated. I believe we ought to think about powerful groups as not losing power so much as considering their need to share it.

I will now talk about national activity. You asked whether there is really national activity in multicultural education. There is national activity, but it's disparate. It's not systemic necessarily. There are good things going on in particular locations. There's the multicultural school that Barbara Shin ran in Minneapolis for a number of years, for example. There's Project REACH in Seattle, Washington, led by Gary Howard (1996), who is the author of a moving and insightful book about his own racial transformation as a White man, *We Can't Teach What We Don't Know* (Howard, 1999). Cherry A. McGee Banks and I worked for three years in the Jackson, Mississippi, public schools to implement a multicultural staff development program, which I think was successful and effective. There are efforts dispersed throughout the nation. In local schools you'll find one or two good teachers, but there are few systemic efforts on a school- or district-wide level.

Making Knowledge Construction Developmentally Appropriate

CROCCO: Given the very decentralized nature of our educational system, that's not surprising; perhaps things that work best are those that start at the grassroots level and build from there. Along those lines, then, the next question has to do with a very particular focus, the classroom and the individual student. I think about this issue in terms of the secondary students I have taught. When you talk about knowledge construction as one of the goals of multicultural education, in my own experience of teaching history I found this commonly done in advanced placement classes. The critique of the textbook representation of the past is a fixed feature of that type of course. However, in developmental terms, at what age is this an appropriate strategy to introduce? Part of the project of maturation is clearly deconstruction of the mythology that we are taught as children. We don't want, however, to produce a nation of cynics and skeptics.

BANKS: I welcome that question. You have a way of asking questions I like and want to talk about because I think they are very important. First, you should remember that I was a fifth-grade teacher before I became a college professor and became involved in the multicultural education project. This is what led me into the project. Whenever I think of knowledge construction, I think of children and teachers, because I see myself first as a teacher and then as a scholar. Let me make a couple of theoretical remarks. I think that knowledge construction clearly has to be related not only to students' cognitive development but also to their moral development. I believe that some things are developmentally appropriate and that others are not. Having said that, I strongly believe that knowledge construction must begin in kindergarten. It has to be related to the child's developmental level. As I thought about your perceptive question, and as I prepared for this interview, I began to think of teaching examples I would use in a kindergarten class.

I think we need to start teaching knowledge construction early because if we don't start teaching it early, by the time students get to my ethnic studies class at the University of Washington—when I show them diverse views of the Western movement—they say they feel they've been cheated. They've been, in effect, betrayed, by this information that has previously been withheld from them.

We have to teach knowledge construction in gradual doses of complexity. I have an example I'd like to share. Let's take the primary grades. Here, we're teaching different and multiple perspectives. We could ask several students to do a simple role play in front of the class. For example, a role play of Pilgrims and the Native Americans meeting or something such as that. Then, after the role play, ask each student to dictate what he or she thought happened. When they're older you can ask them to write their accounts. I've actually done this activity with older students and have had them write their accounts. When they shared their views, they were very different. This activity introduces the idea that we look at the same events and situations differently. We see the same thing but we come up with different views of it. We see the same events differently. Or you could ask the students: What happened in social studies yesterday? You'll get very different views of what happened.

Teaching multiple perspectives is a vehicle for teaching broader conceptualizations and skills. Teaching point-of-view and perspective-taking becomes a vehicle and an effective way to teach thinking skills that are generic to the curriculum. The teacher could tell the students after reading about Thanksgiving to assume that they are Native Americans and then ask them: How do you think the Native Americans felt? How did the Pilgrims feel? We have to be careful about how we do these kinds of activities. I think the *how* becomes really critical, just as important as the *what*. We also have to democratize teaching and implement what I call *equity pedagogy* (equity pedagogy is defined in Chapter 1). We need to actualize in the classroom what bell hooks (1994) calls a pedagogy of freedom.

To summarize, I think knowledge construction has to be developmentally appropriate. It needs to start very early and become increasingly more sophisticated as grade levels increase.

Multicultural Education and Democratic Values

CROCCO: Let me follow up with that because it reminds me of a student teacher who had an unsettling experience this year when she was trying to teach the Holocaust to a group of students who were Latino and African American. She was disturbed because she felt the students were responding with disinterest to the subject matter. In her reconstruction of this classroom incident, she indicated that her students believed the Nazis simply represented a different point of view about the Jews than the way most people feel today. Some might suggest that this is where multiculturalism leads; we will create a group who is adept at perspective taking and yet has lost a moral compass.

BANKS: I like that question because I think it leads to another issue we have to be cognizant of—justice and equality. Multicultural educators are committed to democratic values and believe that not all values are equally good. However, we can't teach democratic values with a stick and coercion. We can best teach democracy by creating a democratic classroom and pedagogy. A friend of mine said that cooperative learning is often taught with a stick and coercion. In one incident, a student asked the teacher, "Do we have to cooperate again today?" This teacher was trying to teach cooperative learning in a way that violated its essence.

CROCCO: Compulsory cooperation.

BANKS: Exactly, and I think we can't really teach democracy with coercion. Democratic values must be an aim of our pedagogy and somehow must be imbued into our discourse, as in Oliver and Shaver (1966) or Kohlberg (Kohlberg & Turiel, 1971). bell hooks (1994) describes democratic teaching as a "pedagogy of freedom" in her book *Teaching to Transgress*. We must help students see that we are committed to democratic values, but we must do this through classroom discourse and conversations. We can ask the students: Is what happened to the Jews consistent with our democratic legacy? Was it consistent with human dignity? Why or why not? I think a democratic ethos has to undergird any perspective-taking pedagogy. Our pedagogy must be grounded in democratic values. That's a very important part of the multicultural project.

CROCCO: That's helpful; thank you.

The Historical Construction of Racist Knowledge

CROCCO: In your book, *Multicultural Education, Transformative Knowledge, and Action* (Banks, 1996c) you talk about earlier ideas on race. For example, you mention Madison Grant; you talk about the Nazis. Do you find this same thread in the anti-multicultural movement of *The Bell Curve* (Herrnstein & Murray, 1994), for example, or in the work *Alien Nation* by Peter Brimelow (1995)? Do you see this new rhetoric as threatening as the earlier manifestations?

BANKS: Not only do I see them as threatening, but I also see them as a continuation of the earlier racist project and movements. As I look at the history of race, not only in America but also in Europe, what I find is that throughout history, throughout every decade, there have been two projects: (1) one to defend the dominant group, through the conceptualization of race and gender in antidemocratic ways, and (2) one to foster liberation, democracy, and justice. What you find in the historical literature is that which of these perspectives becomes legitimate and praised varies enormously with the social, economic, and political context. But both have always coexisted in society. They coexisted, for example, when we had the earliest theories in this country that argued that Jews and African Americans were inferior. We had within the ethnic communities a project that argued that ethnic minorities were not inferior but were equal.

We must take a historical perspective on issues related to race and intellectual ability, as Steven Selden does in his informative and chilling book, *Inheriting Shame: The Story of Eugenics and Racism in America* (Selden, 1999). There's always been a *Bell Curve* existing at some level in society. I think the question we have to ask is why in some times does that perspective become legitimate and why at other times does it becomes less legitimate. Herrnstein wrote an article that foreshadowed *The Bell Curve* in the *Atlantic Monthly* in 1971 (Herrnstein, 1971). He is now deceased. However, his coauthor, Charles Murray, was crowned and celebrated by the national media when their book was published in 1994. Their book (Hernstein & Murray, 1994) was a *New York Times* bestseller for many weeks. Why? Stephen Jay Gould (1994) wondered why in an article in *The New Yorker.* He said it's because of the tendency during this period of "unprecedented ungenerosity" to slash budgets and to deal with the poor harshly. It seems that the people in power can choose which set of data they listen to.

The question is not whether these two conceptions exist. They are always in society. The real questions are: When are they legitimate? How are they treated? Which of these perspectives becomes legitimate and praised? Why did *The Bell Curve* become praised in the 1990s? Jensen was less praised than were Herrnstein and Murray when he published his article in the *Harvard Educational Review* (1969) stating that African Americans have less genetic ability than do Whites. An important question is: Why was Jensen less publicly praised and honored than are Herrnstein and Murray? I think an important part of the answer is the differences in the social context in 1969 and in 1994.

A Conceptual Approach to Multicultural Teaching

CROCCO: That's a very useful answer in explaining many things that happened in history. I like to point out to students that in the 1920s there were more women in U.S. professional schools than in the 1960s. How do you make sense of that? How do you build an argument for vigilance when young women think so much progress has been made? Realizing the duality that you point to gives explanation and reason for continued vigilance; what has been gained can be lost. Again, let me ask you about an issue that surfaces repeatedly. In social studies we teach survey courses that are terribly overloaded. How do you get the stories of diverse groups into an overstuffed curriculum?

BANKS: That's an excellent question. As a teacher, I face the same problem. As one of the authors of a social studies textbook series for a major publisher, we face that problem. Here is how we attempted to deal with that issue in our series. I think our approach makes sense conceptually. We have to recognize that it's a problem that never ends, particularly in history, because there's always more history and a new president. But one way of dealing with it is what we try to do in our series: We select fewer topics and go into greater depth, rather than trying to cover everything. That has a downside, because there are always the people who want you to select everything. But you simply can't teach everything, because history keeps growing. What we've tried to do in the world history program is to select content that illustrates certain key issues and concepts, such as democracy, exploration, revolution, and colonization.

The major concepts, themes, and skills become the driver of the curriculum, not the topics per se. We teach examples of those concepts, such as examining three revolutions—the Mexican, the American, and the French. We deal in depth with those revolutions. That way, if we select three revolutions rather than trying to cover all of them, we can then go into depth. For example, in the United States we can study the 1680 Pueblo revolt in the Southwest. We can study the American Revolution and the French Revolution. We need to remember, as the feminist historian Gerda Lerner reminds us, that it took us 300 years to construct the current paradigm of history that we teach (Lerner, 1997). We're not going to be able to implement the multicultural project in a decade. The second practical way of dealing with this issue is that once we go into depth with fewer key concepts, we can teach diverse perspectives on these key concepts and themes. Let's take the American Revolution, for example. We can examine the perspectives of the people who were loyal to Britain and those who were revolutionaries. Students can also examine the perspective of Native Americans. The American Revolution had some specific effects on Native Americans. The position of African Americans in the American Revolution can be examined. Many African Americans saw the revolution as an opportunity to gain freedom.

Reconstructing America and White Identity

CROCCO: In *Multicultural Education, Transformative Knowledge, and Action* (Banks, 1996c), you discuss racial attitudes about Native Americans in terms of Todorov's (1984) concept of the Other, which delimits both the subject as well as the object. In reading your analysis of Todorov's work, it reminded me of Winthrop Jordan's *White over Black* (1968), and Edmund Morgan's *American Slavery, American Freedom* (1975). If it's true that concepts of the Other serve as ballast for a sense of self for the dominant group, won't it be difficult to dislodge such constructions, since they require not just a new view of the Other, but a new understanding of the self?

BANKS: I think you're exactly right. It's going to be enormously difficult because it does require a new view of self, and also of family, community, and nation. I titled my first Sachs lecture at Teachers College, Columbia University, "Multicultural Education and the Re-Envisioning of America" because I wanted to emphasize that it is essential that this be done to implement the multicultural project and also to focus on how difficult this process is, especially for mainstream groups (Banks, 1996b). That's why I think the works of Robert Carter (1995), Peggy McIntosh (1993), and Gary Howard (1999) on White identity are so important because they focus on reconstructing White identity and American exceptionalism. The work of Michelle Fine and her colleagues on White identity is also significant and informative (Fine, Weis, Powell, & Wong, 1997). Much of White identity is invested in the United States as it has been mythologized: the winning of the West, manifest destiny, and American exceptionalism (White, 1991).

President McKinley exemplifies manifest destiny and American exceptionalism. During the Spanish American War he prayed and asked God what he should do with the Philippines. God told him to annex the Philippines to U.S. territory. Now, of course, the Filipinos' God didn't tell them to do that because they started a rebellion. This is what Joyce Appleby (1992) calls *American exceptionalism.* American exceptionalism is very much tied to White identity. Toni Morrison (1992), in *Playing in the Dark,* describes how White identity was formed in opposition to Blacks.

Yes, the multicultural project does require a reconstruction of White identity and of the notion of American exceptionalism. That's a very difficult psychological project. I think that's why the concept of White identity described by Robert Carter (1995), Peggy McIntosh (1993), and Gary Howard (1999) are critical to helping Whites rethink who they are. I recommend their work highly. For example, McIntosh asks Whites: Do you ever think about going to a store and not being able to find a doll the color of your child? Because Whites tend not to think of themselves as a racial group, it becomes necessary to help Whites to understand that they are a race, like the rest of us. So I think you've touched on something very important but very difficult. Reconstructing White identity and deconstructing the current one are important parts of the project to reform the curriculum in the nation's schools. Peter McLaren (1997) thinks that Whiteness as it exists today must be seriously challenged and transformed.

Creating Caring Classroom Communities

CROCCO: You have said that the goals of multicultural education are *to know, to care, and to act.* This next question picks up on the second item. Since we're addressing teachers here, the practical issue is how do students learn to care? In the same way that you, as a teacher, cannot coerce cooperation, how do you encourage students to care and then to act?

BANKS: I think we have to create a caring community in the classroom. We have to create what psychologists call a superordinate group in the classroom. Let me talk about the work of the late Henry Tajfel (1970; Tajfel & Turner, 1986), a psychologist from the United Kingdom. I have been reviewing his research for a paper I am writing on prejudice reduction. Tajfel's work is important because it is related to what we call *social group identity* or the *minimal group paradigm.* What his research indicates is that people will discriminate on the basis of trivial differences and that people tend to categorize. They tend to categorize groups in terms of in-groups and out-groups. We often think this is because people have experienced a history of discrimination or a history of hostility. But the reason this is called minimal group paradigm is that on the basis of mere categorization of in-group and out-group, people will construct differences based on the most minimal and trivial criteria.

In his research, Tajfel (1970) asked students to estimate the number of dots in a drawing. When he categorized them, they believed they had been put into groups of high-estimators and low-estimators of the dots. He told them they would then be given the opportunity to give rewards. The students discriminated against those who were in the out-group. In some ways this is a depressing finding, because it indicates that people will categorize based on minimal criteria.

Clearly, in order to create a sense of community and to teach students to care, somehow we have to build a superordinate group in the classroom with which all the students can identify. Let me give you one example. If you have a bilingual classroom and only the Mexican American students are speaking Spanish, this tends to intensify in-group versus out-group identity. If, on the other hand, both White and Mexican American students learn Spanish, it becomes the basis for creating a superordinate group. In some ways this may sound contradictory, but it becomes essential: On the one hand we want to help people accept their differences. On the other hand, there's really a need to create community and a superordinate group to which all the students belong. We have to talk about not only ways in which we are different, but also ways in which we are similar. That becomes a real challenge: How do we create a superordinate group, how do we then construct sociologically in the classroom a group so that all kids can see themselves as one? I think a superordinate group identity becomes a prerequisite for caring.

That leads me into the research by Allport (1954), which I want to interject. Allport's theory of group contact suggests ways to create a sense of community. In order to create a sense of community, we first need to create within the group not competition but cooperation. Second, we need to create equal-status situations for the groups. That's a difficult task because often these groups are from very different social-class, ethnic, cultural and language backgrounds that have unequal status within the larger society. Their unequal status is often reproduced in the classroom and in the school.

People interpret what Allport means by equal-status differently. Elizabeth Cohen (Cohen & Roper, 1972) has conceptualized it from a social psychological perspective—equal status means creating a social condition. Let me give you one example of how she's doing this. When she had middle-class White students and working-class African American students in the same classroom she taught the African American students a skill that the White students didn't have in order to create equal status. She taught them how to assemble a transistor radio. She then had them teach that skill to the White students. Now, did this work? She did the transistor radio intervention in some groups and not in others. What happened in the groups that had experienced the intervention? There was more equality of talk. In the groups that did not have the intervention, the White students took over the group conversation.

Allport's other condition is also very important. The contact needs to be sanctioned by authorities, that is, by teachers and principals. A final condition is that the individuals in the contact situation need to become acquainted with each other as human beings. That's a long answer to your question, but I think it's an important question: How do we create a sense of community? I think we do it by creating contact situations that exemplify Allport's conditions. We also create a superordinate group in the contact situation.

Creating an Authentic Unum

CROCCO: It's reminiscent of the work here of Morton Deutsch, a social psychologist who's worked in cooperative learning theory and conflict resolution. The next question asks you to consider the question of community on a much larger scale. You write about the creation of an authentic "unum" with moral authority for the entire nation as part of the endeavor of multicultural education. Do we have a common set of ideals today in the U.S. civic polity that can give that sense of moral authority and help create the *unum*?

BANKS: I think that's a good question as we approach the end of our conversation. The phrase, *E Pluribus Unum,* is our national motto. It is on our coins. The challenge becomes ("pluribus" meaning many people and "unum" meaning one): How do we create a unum that has moral authority for the pluribus? If we don't do that, we have contention, protest, struggle. We have the American Creed values that Myrdal described in *An American Dilemma* (a book worth rereading, published in 1944). Those American Creed values are set down in the founding documents of this nation—the Declaration of Independence, the Constitution, and the Bill of Rights. In order to have an authentic unum, the pluribus must help shape the unum. Historically, the unum has been imposed on the pluribus by a small elite group, and the pluribus has been told that in order to enter the unum, they had to acquire Anglo-Saxon, Protestant, male values.

It's very important to point out that when people argue that they were European-centered values, it wasn't so much Europe—because the Poles' values weren't exemplified in the unum, neither were the Italians'—but it was one group of Europeans, an elite group of Anglo-Saxon Protestants. To create an authentic unum that has moral authority and legitimacy (and by moral authority I mean a unum that people will feel they bought into, feel there's a need for them to respect it, feel that there's a need for them to use it as a guide for their own moral and civic behavior), citizens from diverse ethnic, racial, cultural, and social-class groups have to see that unum as reflecting their struggles, their dreams, their hopes, and their possibilities. It has to be a unum they helped to construct. It has to be a reformulated unum, a transformed unum. Constructing an authentic unum that has moral authority is the way we build a new America to which all of us have allegiance and in which we all have a stake.

CROCCO: It occurs to me that the positive side of this picture is the presence of that rhetoric, of that language, of a set of values found in the national documents that give us a framework for addressing these issues. We are fortunate that we have standards to which we can appeal (that have obviously not been fully implemented) to advance the cause of multicultural education.

BANKS: I'd like to end on a positive note, that yes, the American Creed values give us possibilities for conversation. I recently returned from the United Kingdom, and in some ways we're farther ahead, in part because we have more public dialogue and conversations about race and inequality. The American Creed values are set forth in our nation's founding documents. However, we should acknowledge, as John Hope Franklin (1995) points out, that the founding fathers conceptualized these ideals for an elite because they didn't really trust the pluribus. When they talked about "We the people," they meant Anglo-Saxon males with property. However, the strength of these ideals is their elasticity. They have been enduring because we have been able to expand them to include more and more groups since the Constitution was ratified. A major aim of the multicultural project is to expand for all groups ideals that the founding fathers intended for an elite few.

CHAPTER

9 Multicultural Benchmarks

In this chapter, I summarize and highlight the major components of multicultural education. I also describe benchmarks that you can use to determine the extent to which your school is multicultural, steps that need to be taken to make it more reflective of cultural diversity, and ways to enhance your school's multicultural climate on a continuing basis. Figure 9.1 summarizes the multicultural benchmarks discussed in this chapter.

A Policy Statement

Your school district needs a policy statement on multicultural education that clearly communicates the board of education's commitment to creating and maintaining schools in which students from both gender groups and from diverse racial, ethnic, social-class, cultural, and language groups will have an equal opportunity to learn.

A cogent board of education policy statement will serve several important purposes. It will give legitimacy to multicultural education in the district and thus facilitate the establishment of programs and practices that foster cultural diversity and equal educational opportunities for all students. A board policy statement will also communicate to parents and the public-at-large that multicultural education is a priority in the district.

The board policy statement should include a rationale or justification for multicultural education and guidelines that can be used by the professional and supportive staffs in the district to develop and implement a comprehensive multicultural education plan. In the policy statement adopted by the New York (City) Board of Education (1989), the rationale includes these statements:

> Whereas, people from all parts of the world live and work in New York City, necessitating a multicultural education which fosters intergroup knowledge and understanding and equips students to function effectively in a global society; and Whereas, multicultural education values cultural pluralism and rejects the view that schools should seek to melt away cultural differences or merely tolerate cultural diversity; rather, multicultural education accepts cultural diversity as a valuable resource that should be preserved and extended....

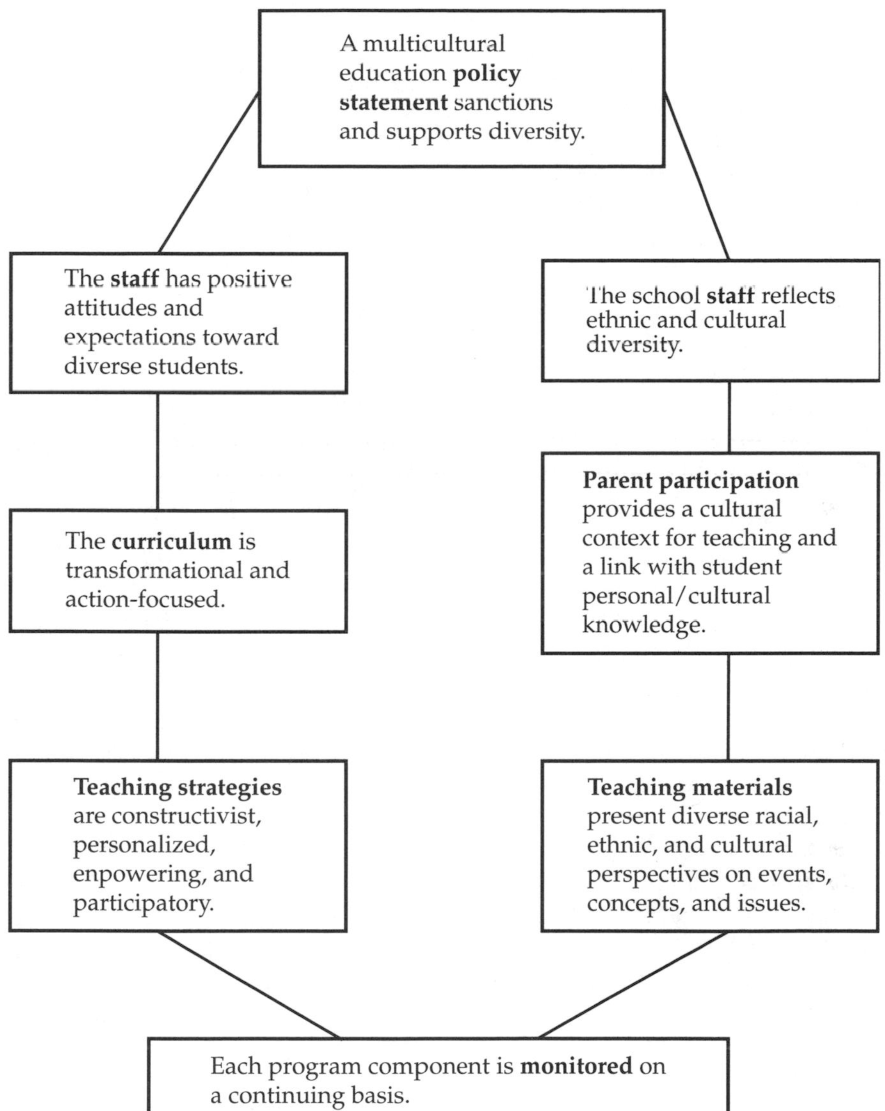

FIGURE 9.1 Multicultural Benchmarks for Assessing and Maintaining an Effective Multicultural School

In 1996, the Indianapolis Public Schools adopted a multicultural education policy similar to that of the New York Board of Education. The Indianapolis policy includes rationale statements as well as three major objectives for multicultural education in the district:

1. To promote and foster intergroup understanding, awareness and appreciation by students and staff of the diverse ethnic, racial, cultural, and linguistic groups represented in the Indianapolis Public Schools, the United States, and the world.
2. To help students develop more positive attitudes toward cultural diversity, especially in early grades by dispelling misconceptions, stereotypes, and negative beliefs about themselves and others.
3. To identify the impact of racism and other barriers to acceptance of differences.

In 1992 the Nebraska legislature enacted a multicultural education bill that requires the state's public schools to implement multicultural education in all core curriculum areas, kindergarten through twelfth grade. The act requires the existing curriculum to incorporate content about the histories and cultures of African Americans, Hispanic Americans, Native Americans, and Asian Americans. The complete text of the Nebraska Multicultural Education Bill is found in Appendix B.

Your school district can model its multicultural policy statement on those developed by the New York Board of Education, the Indianapolis Public Schools, and the Nebraska legislature. Other helpful resources for multicultural education rationales are the position statements developed by national professional organizations, such as the *Curriculum Guidelines for Multicultural Education,* a policy statement adopted by the National Council for the Social Studies (NCSS) (Banks, Cortés, Gay, Garcia, & Ochoa, 1992). The rationale for the NCSS guidelines includes these principles:

1. Ethnic and cultural diversity should be recognized and respected at the individual, group, and societal levels.
2. Ethnic and cultural diversity provides a basis for societal enrichment, cohesiveness, and survival.
3. Equality of opportunity should be afforded to members of all ethnic and cultural groups.
4. Ethnic and cultural identification should be optional for individuals in a democracy. (pp. 4–5)

A publication of the Center for Multicultural Education at the University of Washington, *Diversity within Unity: Essential Principles for Teaching and Learning in a Multicultural Society* (Banks et al., 2001), will be helpful to school districts that are formulating a multicultural education policy statement. This publication also contains a useful checklist that will enable educators to determine the extent to which schools in their district reflect the 12 principles described in *Diversity within Unity.* A summary of the 12 principles—as well as information on how to order the publication or download it online—are found in Appendix A.

The School Staff

The school staff—including administrators, teachers, counselors, and the support staff—should reflect the racial and cultural diversity in U.S. society. The people students see working and interacting in the school environment teach them important lessons about the attitudes of adults toward racial, ethnic, and language diversity. Students need to see administrators, teachers, and counselors from different racial, ethnic, and language backgrounds in order for them to believe that our society values and respects people from different ethnic, racial, and cultural groups. If most of the people students see in powerful and important positions in the school environment are from the dominant racial group, they will have a difficult time developing democratic racial attitudes, no matter how cogent are the words we speak about racial equality. Students' experiences speak much more powerfully than do the words they hear.

School districts should develop and implement a strong policy for the recruitment, hiring, and promotion of people from different racial and ethnic groups. Because most of the nation's teachers are White and female, school districts need to develop and implement innovative and experimental projects to increase the number of students of color who are entering the teaching profession (Brown, Hughes, & Vance, 1999; Ladson-Billings, 2001). A number of school districts have implemented or are participating in such innovative projects. Some of these projects consist of early identification programs in which promising students of color in high school are identified and given incentives for choosing teaching as a career.

Staff Attitudes and Expectations

School districts need to implement continuing staff development programs that help practicing educators to develop high expectations for low-income students and students of color and to better understand the cultural experiences of these students (Banks et al., 2001). An increasing percentage of students in school today are from single-parent homes, have parents with special needs, and have cultural experiences that are dissimilar in significant ways from those of their teachers (Graham, 1992; Hodgkinson, 1991).

Many of these students have health, motivational, and educational needs that often challenge the most gifted and dedicated teachers. Yet many of these students are academically gifted and talented, although their gifts and talents are often not immediately evident and are not revealed by standardized mental ability tests (Fordham, 1996). Their academic gifts and talents are often obscured by skill deficits. Teachers must receive special training to develop the skills and sensitivities needed to perceive the hidden and underdeveloped talent and abilities of a significant number of students of color, language minority students, and low-income students (Ladson-Billings, 2001). Only when they are able to perceive the unrealized talent and potential of these students will teachers be able to increase their expectations for them (McNeil, 2000; Nieto, 2000; Valenzuela, 1999).

Gardner's (1983) theory of *multiple intelligences* can help teachers to reconceptualize the concept of intelligence and to develop a broader view of human ability. This broad view will enable them to see more intellectual strengths in culturally diverse and low-income students. Teachers should also use multiple culturally sensitive techniques to assess the complex cognitive and social skills of students who belong to diverse cultural, language and social-class groups (Armour-Thomas & Gopaul-McNicol, 1998).

Creating successful experiences for students of color will enable them to develop a high self-concept of academic ability as well as enable their teachers to increase their academic expectations for them (Brookover & Erickson, 1969). Student behavior and teacher expectations are related in an interactive way. The more teachers expect from students academically, the more they are likely to achieve; the more academically successful students are, the higher teacher expectations are likely to be for them (Brophy & Good, 1970; Rosenthal & Jacobson, 1968).

The Curriculum

The school curriculum should be reformed so that students will view concepts, events, issues, and problems from different ethnic perspectives and points of view (Banks, 1997b; Banks, 2001). Reconceptualizing the curriculum and making ethnic content an integral part of a transformed curriculum should be distinguished from merely adding ethnic content to the curriculum. Ethnic content can be added to the curriculum without transforming it or changing its basic assumptions, perspectives, and goals.

Content about Native Americans can be added to a Eurocentric curriculum that teaches students that Columbus discovered America. In such a curriculum, the students will read about Columbus's view of the Native Americans when he "discovered" them. In a transformed curriculum in which content about Native Americans is an integral part, the interaction of Columbus and Native Americans would not be conceptualized as Columbus "discovering" Native Americans (Bigelow & Peterson, 1998; Zinn, 2001). Rather, students would read about the culture of the Arawak Indians (also called *Tainos*) as it existed in the late 1400s (Olsen, 1974; Rouse, 1992), the journey of Columbus, and the meeting of the aboriginal American and European cultures in the Caribbean in 1492 (Josephy, 1992).

"Discovery" is not an accurate way to conceptualize and view the interaction of Columbus and the Arawaks unless this interaction is viewed exclusively from the point of view of Columbus and other Europeans. "The Meeting of Two Old World Cultures" is a more appropriate way to describe the Arawak-Columbus encounter. It is imperative that the encounter be viewed from the perspectives of the Arawaks or Tainos (Golden, McConnell, Mueller, Poppen, & Turkovich, 1991; Ponce de Leon, 1992; Stannard, 1992), in addition to that of Columbus and the Europeans (Morison, 1974). Excellent materials are available that teachers can use to teach diverse views of the Arawak-Columbus encounter. These materials include the special issue of the *National Geographic* (1991) on "America Before Columbus;" *Morning Girl,* a story by Michael Dorris (1992) about a twelve-year-old Taino who lives on a Bahamian island in 1492; *Rethinking Columbus: The Next 500* years by Bigelow and Peterson (1998), and "Columbus and Western Civilization," an informative and powerful essay by Howard Zinn (2001) in *Howard Zinn on History,* a collection of his essays.

The multicultural curriculum not only helps students to view issues and problems from diverse ethnic perspectives and points of view, but it is also conceptual, interdisciplinary, and decision-making focused (see Chapter 6). It helps students to make decisions on important issues and to take effective personal and civic action (Banks & Banks, 1999).

The multicultural curriculum is a *dynamic process;* it is not possible to create a multicultural curriculum, hand it to teachers, and claim that a multicultural curriculum exists in the district. The teacher's role in its implementation is an integral part of a multicultural curriculum. The teacher mediates the curriculum with her or his values, perspectives, and teaching styles. Although multicultural materials are essential for implementing a multicultural curriculum, they are ineffective when used by a teacher who lacks a knowledge base in multicultural education or who does not have positive and clarified attitudes toward a range of racial, ethnic, language, and cultural groups. A well-designed, continuing staff development program is essential for the development and implementation of an effective multicultural curriculum (Ladson-Billings, 2001).

An effective preservice teacher education program is also essential for the successful implementation of multicultural education in the schools. School districts should demand that teacher education institutions have a strong multicultural education component in their programs as a condition for the employment of their graduates. The National Council for the Accreditation of Teacher Education has taken a leadership role in multicultural education by requiring its members to include multicultural education outcomes in their teacher education programs (National Council for the Accreditation of Teacher Education [NCATE], 1997). A large number of the nation's teacher education institutions are members of NCATE.

Teaching Strategies

The multicultural curriculum should be implemented with teaching strategies that are involving, interactive, personalized, and cooperative. The teacher should listen to and legitimize the voices of students from different racial, cultural, and gender groups. Multicultural content is inherently emotive, personal, conflictual, and interactive. Consequently, it is essential that students be given ample opportunities to express their feelings and emotions, to interact with their peers and classmates, and to express rage or pride when multicultural issues are discussed.

Didactic, teacher-centered instruction has serious disadvantages when teaching any kind of content. However, it is especially inappropriate when teaching multicultural content, an area in which diversity is valued and different perspectives are an integral part of the content. Students must be taught the skills needed to talk about race in civil, meaningful, and thoughtful ways. Conflict resolution and intergroup dialogue (Zúñiga & Nagda, 1993) are skills that can be taught to students.

Teaching Materials

School districts need to develop and implement a policy for selecting teaching materials that describe the historical and contemporary experiences of various ethnic, language, and cultural groups and that present issues, problems, and concepts from the perspectives of these groups. It is not sufficient for textbooks and other teaching materials merely to include content about various ethnic, language, and cultural groups. The content about ethnic and cultural groups should be an integral part of the textbook or presentation and not an add-on or appendage. It is not uncommon for content about people of color and women to be added to a textbook in a special section, as a special feature, or with photographs.

When ethnic content is placed in teaching materials primarily as add-ons or appendages, the text or presentation has not been reconceptualized or reformed in a way that will allow students to rethink the mainstream American metanarrative, to challenge their personal assumptions, or to develop new perspectives and insights on U.S. history and culture. If ethnic content is added to teaching materials and viewed from Anglocentric perspectives and points of view—which often happens—then ethnic stereotypes and misconceptions held by students are likely to be reinforced rather than reduced. How ethnic content is integrated into textbooks and other teaching materials is as important as, if not more important than, whether it is included.

Disproportionality

A major goal of multicultural education is to create equal educational opportunities for students from different racial, ethnic, language, and social-class groups (see Chapter 4). The gaps in academic achievement, drop-out, and graduation rates for students from different racial and income groups are enormous in most school districts. Each school district needs to determine the gaps in academic achievement, drop-out rates, and graduation rates for students from different racial, language, and income groups. Each district also needs to develop a comprehensive and well-conceptualized plan for closing these gaps.

Special attention should also be given to the proportion of students of color that is expelled or suspended from school, and the percentage that is enrolled in special education and in classes for gifted students (Artiles & Zamora-Durán, 1997; Sapon-Shevin, 1994; Zigmond, 1992). In most school districts, students of color—especially males—are overrepresented among the students who are suspended from school and in classes for the mentally retarded (Reschly, 1988). However, these students are usually underrepresented in classes for gifted students (Ford, 1996).

A goal of each school district should be to have students from different racial, language, and social-class groups represented in special education and in gifted classes roughly equal to their percentage in their district's population. This means that the percentage of students of color in special education would be reduced and their percentage in classes for gifted students would increase in most school districts.

Parent Involvement

Because of the enormity of the problems faced by schools today, it is not likely that the school can succeed in its major missions—helping students to attain academic skills and to become effective citizens of a democratic society—unless it can solicit the support of parents and the public-at-large (Comer et al., 1996; Graham, 1992; Hidalgo, Bright, Siu, Swap, & Epstein, 1995). However, soliciting the support of parents is a tremendous challenge for schools in today's society. Increasingly within the United States both parents work outside the home. According to *Education Week* (Here They Come, Ready or Not, May 14, 1986), fewer than 5 percent of U.S. households now conform to the standard-model family of past decades—a working father, mother at home, and two or more school-age children.

Other institutions are increasingly taking on functions that were in the past the primary responsibility of families. Because of the tremendous changes within U.S. society, we need to rethink the idea of parent involvement and reconceptualize ways in which parents can support the school, given the other demands now being made on their time (Comer, 1980). Asking a parent to provide a place for his or her child to study, to monitor the child's TV watching, and to restrict it to one hour per day may be a limited involvement, but it may be the only kind of parent involvement that the school can realistically expect from many parents who care deeply about their children's education.

Educators should be careful not to equate noninvolvement in traditional ways in school as lack of parent interest or lack of participation. Also, many parents are reluctant to get involved with schools because they lack a sense of empowerment and believe that their opinion will not matter anyway. Other parents are reluctant to become involved with schools because of their painful memories of their own school days. School districts should conceptualize and implement a program for involving parents in school that is consistent with the changing characteristics of families, parents, and society (C. A. M. Banks, 2001; Graham, 1992; Hodgkinson, 1991).

Monitoring

The successful implementation and improvement of a multicultural education program within a school or district require an effective monitoring plan. Ways must be developed to determine whether (1) the multicultural education goals established by the board of education are being attained, (2) steps that need to be taken to close the gap between the goals and actual program implementation, and (3) incentives that are needed to motivate people in the district to participate in the efforts being undertaken to attain the district's multicultural education goals and objectives.

An effective monitoring program may include (1) classroom visitations to determine the extent to which the content and strategies used by teachers are consistent with the cultural and language characteristics of students; (2) examination of standardized test scores disaggregated by race, social class, and language groups; and (3) examination of the percentage of students of color who are suspended, are dropouts, and who are classified as mentally retarded and gifted.

The monitoring program should not focus on specific individuals, such as teachers and principals, but should be systemic and focus on the total school as a unit. A systemic approach to monitoring will weaken resistance to a comprehensive monitoring program as well as reinforce the idea that multicultural education is a shared responsibility of the school and that everyone within the school building has a stake in its successful implementation, including the principal and teachers, as well as other members of the professional and support staffs, such as the secretary, the custodian, and the bus driver.

An effective and well-conceptualized monitoring program will provide the feedback needed to determine whether the benchmarks described in this chapter are being realized in your school, and the steps that need to be taken to ensure the ongoing improvement of its multicultural climate. The *Multicultural Education Evaluation Checklist* in Appendix D is designed to help you assess the environment of your school and to plan and implement action to make it more consistent with the multicultural realities of the United States and the world.

GLOSSARY

Afrocentric Explanations, cultural characteristics, teaching materials, and other factors related to the heritages, histories, and cultures of people of African descent who live in the United States and in other parts of the world. The 2000 U.S. Census indicated that there were approximately 35 million African Americans living in the United States.

Anglocentric Explanations, cultural characteristics, teaching materials, and other factors related the heritages, histories, and cultures of Whites of British descent in the United States.

Canon A standard or criterion used to define, select, and evaluate knowledge in the school and university curriculum within a nation. The list of book-length works or readings selected using the standard is also described as the *canon.* Historically in the United States, the *canon* that has dominated the curriculum has been Eurocentric and male-oriented.

Culture The ideations, symbols, behaviors, values, and beliefs that are shared by a human group. Culture may also be defined as the symbols, institutions, or other components of human societies that are created by human groups to meet their survival needs.

Ethnic group A group that shares a common history, a sense of peoplehood and identity, values, behavioral characteristics, and a communication system. The members of an ethnic group usually view their group as distinct and separate from other cultural groups within a society. Ethnic groups within the United States include Anglo Americans, Irish Americans, Polish Americans, and German Americans.

Ethnic minority group An ethnic group that has unique behavioral and/or racial characteristics that enable other groups to easily identify its members. These groups are often a numerical minority within the nation-state and the victims of institutionalized discrimination. Jewish Americans are an example of an ethnic group differentiated on the basis of cultural and religious characteristics. African Americans, Mexican Americans, and Japanese Americans are differentiated on the basis of both biological and cultural characteristics.

The term *ethnic minority group* is being used increasingly less within U.S. educational communities because of the nation's changing racial, ethnic, and language characteristics. In many of the nation's major cities, such as Los Angeles, Detroit, New York, and Chicago, students of color make up majorities rather than minorities in the public school population. The U.S. Census projects that by the year 2050 Whites will make up only 52.5 percent of the nation's population. Consequently, the nation will be made up of groups of minorities. The term *people of color* is increasingly replacing ethnic minority group in educational discourse in the United States.

Ethnic-specific programs Curricula and educational policies that focus on one designated ethnic group, such as Anglo Americans, Latino Americans, or Asian Americans, rather than on a range of ethnic and cultural groups.

Ethnic studies The scientific and humanistic study of the histories, cultures, and experiences of ethnic groups within the United States and in other societies.

Eurocentric explanations Cultural characteristics, teaching materials, and other factors related to the heritages, histories, and cultures of people of European descent who live in the United States and in other nations.

Global education The study of the cultures, institutions, and interconnectedness of nations outside of the United States. *Global education* is often confused with multicultural education, which deals with educational issues in the United States or within another nation. Global education deals with issues, problems, and developments outside of the United States or outside another nation.

Knowledge construction The process that helps students understand how social, behavioral, and natural scientists create knowledge, and how their implicit cultural assumptions, frames of references, perspectives, cultural contexts, and biases influence the knowledge they construct. Knowledge construction teaching strategies, which are constructivist, involve students in activities that enable them to create their own interpretations of the past, present, and future.

Multicultural education An educational reform movement whose major goal is to restructure curricula and educational institutions so that students from diverse social-class, racial, and ethnic groups—as well as both gender groups—will experience equal educational opportunities. Multicultural education consists of three major components: (1) an educational reform movement whose aim is to create equal educational opportunities for all students; (2) an ideology whose aim is to actualize American democratic ideals, such as equality, justice, and human rights; and (3) a process that never ends because there will always be a discrepancy between democratic ideals and school and societal practices.

Multiculturalists A group of theorists, researchers, and educators who believe that the curricula within the nation's schools, colleges, and universities should be reformed so that they reflect the experiences and perspectives of the diverse cultures and groups in U.S. society.

Multiethnic education An educational reform movement designed to restructure educational institutions so that students from diverse ethnic groups, such as Asian Americans, Native Americans, and Latinos, will experience equal educational opportunities. This term was used frequently in the 1970s but is rarely used in educational discourse today.

Paradigm An interrelated set of facts, concepts, generalizations, and theories that attempt to explain human behavior or a social phenomenon and that imply policy and action. A paradigm, which is also a set of explanations, has specific goals, assumptions, and values that can be described. Paradigms compete with one another in the arena of ideas and educational policy. Explanations such as *at-risk students, culturally deprived students,* and *culturally different students* are paradigms.

Paradigm shift The process that occurs when an individual accepts and internalizes an explanation or theory to explain a phenomenon or event that differs substantially from the one that he or she previously had internalized. An example occurs when an individual who previously believed that Columbus discovered America now views the Columbus-Arawak encounter as the meeting of two old-world cultures.

People of color A term used to refer to racial groups in the United States that have historically experienced institutionalized discrimination and racism because of their physical characteristics. These groups include African Americans, Asian Americans, Latinos, Native Americans, and Native Hawaiians.

Powerful ideas Key concepts or themes—such as culture, socialization, power, and discrimination—that are used to organize lessons, units, and courses. In conceptual teaching, instruction focuses on helping students to see relationships and to derive principles and generalizations.

Transformative curriculum A curriculum that challenges the basic assumptions and implicit values of the Eurocentric, male-dominated curriculum institutionalized in U.S. schools, colleges, and universities. It helps students to view concepts, events, and situations from diverse racial, ethnic, gender, and social-class perspectives. The *transformative curriculum* also helps students to construct their own interpretations of the past, present, and future.

Western traditionalists Social scientists, historians, and other scholars who argue that the European Western tradition should be at the center of the curriculum in U.S. schools, colleges, and universities because of the cogent influence that Western ideas and ideals have had on the development of the United States and the world.

APPENDIX A

Essential Principles for Teaching and Learning in a Multicultural Society[1]

What do we know about education and diversity and how do we know it? This two-part question guided the Multicultural Education Consensus Panel that was sponsored by the Center for Multicultural Education at the University of Washington and the Common Destiny Alliance at the University of Maryland. The findings of the Consensus Panel are the product of a four-year project during which the panel reviewed and synthesized research related to diversity. The panel's work was supported by a grant from the Carnegie Corporation of New York. The panel members are specialists in race relations and multicultural education. An interdisciplinary group, it was made up of two psychologists, a political scientist, a sociologist, and four multicultural education specialists. The panel was modeled after the consensus panels that develop and write reports for the National Research Council of the National Academy of Sciences. In National Research Council panels, an expert group decides, based on research and practice, what is known about a particular problem and the most effective actions that can be taken to solve it.

The findings of the Multicultural Education Consensus Panel, which are called *essential principles*, describe ways in which educational policy and practice related to diversity can be improved. These principles are derived from research and practice. They are designed to help educational practitioners in all types of schools increase student academic achievement and improve intergroup skills. Another aim is to help schools successfully meet the challenges of and benefit from the diversity that characterizes the United States and its schools. A summary of the 12 essential principles identified by the Consensus Panel follow. Readers can

[1]Reprinted with permission from James A. Banks, Peter Cookson, Geneva Gay, Willis D. Hawley, Jacqueline Jordan Irvine, Sonia Nieto, Janet Ward Schofield, and Walter G. Stephan (2001). *Diversity within Unity: Essential Principles for Teaching and Learning in a Multicultural Society.* Seattle: Center for Multicultural Education, University of Washington.

Information for ordering this publication and for downloading it can be obtained on the center's website: http://depts.washington.edu/centerme/home.htm

examine *Diversity within Unity*, the publication in which the design principles are described, on-line as well as order the publication from the Center for Multicultural Education, University of Washington, Seattle. Online and ordering information is at the bottom of page 125.

Teacher Learning

Principle 1: Professional development programs should help teachers understand the complex characteristics of ethnic groups within U.S. society and the ways in which race, ethnicity, language, and social class interact to influence student behavior.

Student Learning

Principle 2: Schools should ensure that all students have equitable opportunities to learn and to meet high standards.

Principle 3: The curriculum should help students understand that knowledge is socially constructed and reflects researchers' personal experiences as well as the social, political, and economic contexts in which they live and work.

Principle 4: Schools should provide all students with opportunities to participate in extra- and cocurricular activities that develop knowledge, skills, and attitudes that increase academic achievement and foster positive interracial relationships.

Intergroup Relations

Principle 5: Schools should create or make salient superordinate crosscutting group memberships in order to improve intergroup relations.

Principle 6: Students should learn about stereotyping and other related biases that have negative effects on racial and ethnic relations.

Principle 7: Students should learn about the values shared by virtually all cultural groups (e.g., justice, equality, freedom, peace, compassion, and charity).

Principle 8: Teachers should help students acquire the social skills needed to interact effectively with students from other racial, ethnic, cultural, and language groups.

Principle 9: Schools should provide opportunities for students from different racial, ethnic, cultural, and language groups to interact socially under conditions designed to reduce fear and anxiety.

School Governance, Organization, and Equity

Principle 10: A school's organizational strategies should ensure that decision-making is widely shared and that members of the school community learn collaborative skills and dispositions in order to create a caring environment for students.

Principle 11: Leaders should develop strategies that ensure that all public schools, regardless of their locations, are funded equitably.

Assessment

Principle 12: Teachers should use multiple culturally sensitive techniques to assess complex cognitive and social skills.

APPENDIX B

Nebraska Multicultural Education Bill

Legislature of Nebraska, Ninety-Second Legislative, Second Session, Legislature Bill 922, Final Reading

Introduced by Chambers, 11; Landis, 46; Schimek, 27; Nelson, 35
Read First Time January 8, 1992

Committee: Education

A Bill

FOR AN ACT relating to schools and school districts; to amend section 79-4, 140.16, Revised Statutes Supplement, 1990; to define a term; to provide for the development and implementation of multicultural education programs as prescribed; to provide powers and duties for school districts and the State Department of Education; to provide for rules and regulations; to harmonize provisions; to eliminate provisions requiring duties to be performed by a certain date; and to repeal the original section. Be it enacted by the State of Nebraska.

Section 1. For purposes of section 1 to 5 of this act, multicultural education shall include but not be limited to, studies relative to the culture, history, and contributions of African Americans, Hispanic Americans, Native Americans, and Asian Americans. Special emphasis shall be placed on human relations and sensitivity toward all races.

Section 2. (1) Each school district, in consultation with the State Department of Education, shall develop for incorporation into all phases of the curriculum of grades kindergarten through twelve a multicultural education program.

(2) The department shall create and distribute recommended multicultural education curriculum guidelines to all school districts. Each district shall create its own multicultural education program based on such recom-

mended guidelines. Each program shall be approved by the department, and a copy of each such program shall be on file with the department.

(3) The multicultural education program shall be a part of the curriculum of each district beginning in the school year 1993–94 and each school year thereafter.

(4) The incorporation of the multicultural education program into the curriculum of each district shall not change (a) the number of instructional hours prescribed for elementary and high school students or (b) the number of instructional hours dedicated to the existing curriculum of each district.

Section 3. (1) Each school shall present evidence annually, in a form prescribed by the State Department of Education, to the department that multicultural education is being taught to students pursuant to section 2 of this act. The department shall evaluate the effectiveness of the multicultural education program and establish reasonable timelines for the submission of such evidence.

(2) A school district which fails to provide or fails to provide evidence annually of multicultural education pursuant to section 2 of this act shall lose accreditation status.

Section 4. In conjunction with the multicultural education program prescribed in section 2 of this act, the State Department of Education shall design an authentic assessment system to assess student cultural awareness and sensitivity. The baseline assessment shall be conducted during the first quarter of the 1993–94 school year. A second assessment shall be administered to the same districts during the first quarter of the 1997–1998 school year to measure effectiveness of the multicultural education programs. The department shall publish the results of each assessment to the Legislature, the State Board of Education, and each school district. Beginning with school year 2002–2003 and each five school years thereafter, the department shall conduct assessments in the manner prescribed in this section to monitor student cultural awareness and sensitivity.

Section 5. The State Department of Education shall adopt and promulgate rules and regulations to carry out sections 1 to 4 of this act.

Section 6. That section 79-4, 140.16, Revised Statutes Supplement, 1900, be amended to read as follows:

79-4, 140.16. (1) To ensure both equality of opportunity and quality of programs offered all public schools in the state shall be required to meet quality and performance-based approval and accreditation standards as prescribed by the State Board of Education. The board shall establish a core curriculum standard, which shall include multicultural education and vocational education courses, for all public schools in the state. Accreditation and approval standards shall be designed to assure effective schooling and quality of instructional programs regardless of school size, wealth, or geographic location. The board shall recognize and encourage the maximum use of cooperative programs and may provide for approval or accreditation of programs on a cooperative basis, including the sharing of administrative and instructional staff, between school districts for the purpose of meeting the approval and accreditation requirements established pursuant to this section and section 79-328.

(2) The Commissioner of Education shall appoint an accreditation committee which shall be representative of the educational institutions and agencies of the state and shall include as a member the director of admissions of the University of Nebraska.

(3) The accreditation committee shall be responsible for: (a) Recommending appropriate standards and policies with respect to the accreditation and classification of schools; and (b) making recommendations annually to the commissioner relative to the accreditation and classification of individual schools. No school shall be considered for accreditation status which has not first fulfilled all requirements for an approved school.

(4) By school year 1993–94 all public schools in the state shall be accredited.

(5) It is the intent of the Legislature that all public school students shall have access to all educational services required of accredited schools. Such services may be provided through cooperative programs or alternative methods of delivery.

Section. 7. That original section 79-4, 140.16, Revised Statutes Supplement, 1990, is repealed.

APPENDIX C

Checklist for Evaluating Informational Materials

Criteria Questions	Rating Hardly at all ⟷ Extensively					
1. Includes a range of racial, ethnic, and cultural groups that reflects the diversity within U.S. life and society.						
2. Describes the wide range of diversity that exists within racial, ethnic, and cultural groups (for example, social class, regional, ideology, and language diversity within ethnic groups).						
3. Describes the roles, experiences, challenges and contributions of women within various racial and ethnic groups.						
4. Helps students to view American history and society from the perspectives of women within various racial and ethnic groups, such as African American women who played major roles in the Civil Rights Movement but who are often not given much visibility compared to men in the movement (e.g., Ella Baker, Jo Ann Gipson Robinson, and Fannie Lou Hammer).						
5. Describes the range of dialects and languages within U.S. society, the problems of language minority groups, and the contributions that diverse languages make to U.S. society.						
6. Integrates the histories and experiences of racial and ethnic groups into the mainstream story of the development of America rather than isolating them into special sections, boxes, and features.						
7. Challenges the concepts of American exceptionalism and manifest destiny and helps students to develop new views of the development of the United States.						

Criteria Questions	Rating Hardly at all ⟷ Extensively					
8. Helps students to view the historical development of the United States from the perspectives of groups that have been victimized in American history (such as Native Americans, Mexican Americans and African Americans, and lower socioeconomic groups); and from the perspectives of groups that have been advantaged in America, such as Anglo Saxon Protestants and higher-income groups.						
9. Uses primary resources to document and describe the experiences of racial, ethnic, and cultural groups in the United States.						
10. Helps students to understand the powerful role of social class in U.S. society and the extent to which class is still a significant factor in determining the life chances of U.S. citizens.						
11. Helps students to understand the extent to which *acculturation* within U.S. society is a two-way process and the ways in which majority groups have incorporated (and sometimes appropriated) aspects of the cultures of ethnic groups of color and the extent to which ethnic groups of color have adapted and incorporated mainstream culture into their ways of life.						
12. Helps students to understand the extent to which the American dream of equality for all citizens is still incomplete and the role that students need to play to help close the gap between American democratic ideals and realities.						
13. The mathematics and science materials help students to understand the ways in which the assumptions, perspectives, and problems within these fields are often culturally based and influenced.						
14. The mathematics and science materials describe the ways in which these disciplines influence the knowledge that is constructed about racial, ethnic, cultural, and gender groups.						

Criteria Questions	Rating Hardly at all ⟷ Extensively					
15. The mathematics and science materials help students to understand the ways in which people from a variety of cultures and groups have contributed to the development of scientific and mathematical knowledge.						
16. Acquaints students with key concepts that are essential for understanding the history and cultures of racial, ethnic, and cultural groups in the United States, such as prejudice, discrimination, institutionalized racism, institutionalized sexism, and social-class stratification.						
17. Acquaints students with key historical and cultural events that are essential for understanding the experiences of racial and ethnic groups in the United States, such as the Harlem Renaissance, the Middle Passage, the internment of Japanese Americans, the Treaty of Guadalupe Hidalgo, and the Trail of Tears.						

APPENDIX D

A Multicultural Education Evaluation Checklist

Criteria Questions	Rating Hardly at all ⟷ Extensively		
1. Does school policy reflect the ethnic, cultural, and gender diversity in U.S. society?			
2. Is the total school culture (including the hidden curriculum) multiethnic and multicultural?			
3. Do the learning styles favored by the school reflect the learning styles of the students?			
4. Does the school reflect and sanction the range of languages and dialects spoken by the students and within the larger society?			
5. Does the school involve parents from diverse ethnic and cultural groups in school activities, programs, and planning?			
6. Does the counseling program of the school reflect the ethnic diversity in U.S. society?			
7. Are the testing procedures used by the school multicultural and ethnically fair?			
8. Are instructional materials examined for ethnic, cultural, and gender bias?			
9. Are the formalized curriculum and course of study multiethnic and multicultural? Do they help students to view events, situations, and concepts from diverse ethnic and cultural perspectives and points of view?			
10. Do the teaching styles and motivational systems in the school reflect the ethnic and cultural diversity of the student body?			
11. Are the attitudes, perceptions, beliefs, and behavior of the total staff ethnically and racially sensitive?			

Criteria Questions	Rating Hardly at all ←→ Extensively		
12. Does the school have systematic, comprehensive, mandatory, and continuing multicultural staff development programs?			
13. Is the school staff (administrative, instructional, counseling, and supportive) multiethnic and multicultural?			
14. Is the total atmosphere of the school positively responsive to racial, ethnic, cultural, and language differences?			
15. Do school assemblies and holidays reflect the ethnic and cultural diversity in U.S. society?			
16. Does the school lunch program prepare meals that reflect the range of ethnic foods eaten in the U.S.?			
17. Do the bulletin boards, physical education program, music, and other displays and activities in the school reflect ethnic and cultural diversity?			

Source: Adapted from J. A. Banks (1981). Multiethnic education and school reform. In L. V. Edinger, P. L. Houts, & D. V. Meyer (Eds.), *Education in the 80s: Curricular Challenges* (pp. 112–123). Washington, DC: National Education Association.

APPENDIX E

A Multicultural Education Basic Library

Books

Banks, J. A. (Ed.). (1996-continuing). *Multicultural Education Series.* A series of books—written by authors from diverse racial and ethnic groups—that focus on research, theory, and practice in multicultural education. Teachers College Press, Columbia University, 1234 Amsterdam Avenue, New York, NY 10027. Authors include Gary Howard, Sonia Nieto, Carlos E. Cortés, and Guadalupe Valdes. Website: www.teacherscollegepress.com

Banks, J. A. (1997). *Teaching strategies for ethnic studies* (6th ed.). Boston: Allyn & Bacon.

Banks, J. A., & Banks, C. A. M. (Eds.). (2001). *Handbook of research on multicultural education.* San Francisco: Jossey-Bass.

Banks, J. A., & Banks, C. A. M. (Eds.). (2001). *Multicultural education: Issues and perspectives* (4th ed.). New York: Wiley.

Banks, J. A., Cookson, P., Gay, G., Hawley, W. D., Irvine, J. J., Nieto, S., Schofield, J. W., & Stephan, W. G. (2001). *Diversity within unity: Essential principles for teaching and learning in a multicultural society.* Seattle: Center for Multicultural Education, University of Washington.

Gay, G. (2000). *Culturally responsive teaching: Theory, research and practice.* New York: Teachers College Press.

Grant, C. A., & Ladson-Billings, G. (Eds.). (1997). *Dictionary of multicultural education.* Phoenix, AZ: The Oryx Press.

Howard, G. (1999). *We can't teach what we don't know: White teachers, multiracial schools.* New York: Teachers College Press.

Muse, D. (Ed.). (1997). *The New Press guide to multicultural resources for young readers.* New York: The New Press.

Nieto, S. (1999). *The light in their eyes: Creating multicultural learning communities.* New York. Teachers College Press.

Stephan, W. (1999). *Reducing prejudice and stereotyping in schools.* New York: Teachers College Press.

Takaki, R. (1993). *A different mirror: A history of multicultural America.* Boston: Little Brown.

Journals and Magazines

Multicultural Perspectives, an official journal of the National Association for Multicultural Education. Published four times a year by Lawrence Erlbaum Associates, Inc., 10 Industrial Avenue, Mahwah, NJ 07430.

MultiCultual Review, published quarterly by GP Subscription, an imprint of Greenwood Publishing Group, Inc., 88 Post Rd., W., P.O. Box 5007, Westport, CT 06881-5007. A comprehensive source of reviews of books for children and youth that deal with racial, ethnic, cultural, and religious groups.

Teaching Tolerance, a magazine published twice a year by Teaching Tolerance, a division of the Southern Poverty Law Center, 400 Washington Avenue, Montgomery, AL 36104. Distributed free to school and university educators. Teaching Tolerance also produces and distributes excellent videotapes that can be used in schools and for teacher education courses. Teaching Tolerance also has a website: http://www.splcenter.org/teachingtolerance

Catalogs

Anti-Defamation League Resources for Classroom and Community. An excellent and comprehensive catalog of books, videotapes, posters, and other materials for use in the multicultural classroom and school. Published annually. Anti-Defamation League, 823 United Nations Plaza, New York, NY 10017.

Arte Público Press Catalog. Arte Público Press is the oldest and largest publisher of U.S. Hispanic literature. A catalog of fiction, poetry, drama, literary criticism, and art by leading figures in Mexican American, Puerto Rican, Cuban, and U.S. Hispanic literature. Includes books for children and young people. University of Houston, Houston, TX 77204–2090. Published annually, with supplements during the year.

Lee & Low Books Catalog. Lee & Low Books publishes multicultural literature for children. 95 Madison Avenue, New York, NY 10016. Published annually with supplements.

Multicultural Studies. A catalog of the Social Studies School Services, Culver City, California. A comprehensive collection of books, posters, videotapes and other materials for the diverse classroom. Web site: http://www.socialstudies.com

REFERENCES

Aboud, F. (1988). *Children & prejudice*. Cambridge, MA: Blackwell Publishers.

Allen, P. G. (1986). *The sacred hoop: Recovering the feminine in American Indian traditions*. Boston: Beacon Press.

Allport, G. W. (1954). *The nature of prejudice*. Cambridge, MA: Addison-Wesley.

American Association for the Advancement of Science. (1989). *Science for all Americans: A project 2061 report on literacy goals in science, mathematics, and technology*. Washington, DC: Author.

Anderson, M. L., & Collins, P. H. (Eds.). (1992). *Race, class, and gender: An anthology*. Belmont, CA: Wadsworth.

Anyon, J. (1997). *Ghetto schooling: A political economy of urban educational reform*. New York: Teachers College Press.

Anzaldua, G. (1999). *Borderlands: The New Mestiza*. San Francisco: Spinsters/Aunt Lute.

Apple, M. W. (1993). *Official knowledge: Democratic education in a conservative age*. New York: Routledge.

Apple, M. W., & Christian-Smith, L. K. (Eds.). (1991). *The politics of the textbook*. New York: Routledge.

Applebee, A. N. (1993). *Literature in the secondary school: Studies of curriculum and instruction*. Urbana, IL: National Council of Teachers of English.

Appleby, J. (1992). Recovering America's historic diversity: Beyond exceptionalism. *The Journal of American History*, 79(2), 419–431.

Apter, D. E. (1977). Political life and cultural pluralism. In M. M. Tumin & W. Plotch (Eds.), *Pluralism in a democratic society* (pp. 5–91). New York: Praeger.

Armitage, S. (1987). Through women's eyes: A new view of the west. In S. Armitage & E. Jameson (Eds.), *The women's west* (pp. 9–18). Norman: University of Oklahoma Press.

Armour-Thomas, E., & Gopaul-McNicol, S. (1998). *Assessing intelligence: Applying a bio-cultural model*. Thousand Oaks, CA: Sage.

Arnove, R. E. (1999). Reframing comparative education: The dialectic of the global and the local. In R. F. Amove & C. A. Torres (Eds.), *Comparative education: The dialectic of the global and the local* (pp. 1–23). New York: Rowman & Littlefield.

Aronson, E., & Gonzalez, A. (1988). Desegregation, jigsaw, and the Mexican-American experience. In P. A. Katz & D. A. Taylor (Eds.), *Eliminating racism: Profiles in controversy* (pp. 301–314). New York: Plenum.

Artiles, A. J., & Zamora-Durán, G. (Eds.). (1997). *Reducing disproportionate representation of culturally diverse students in special and gifted education*. Reston, VA: The Council for Exceptional Children.

Asante, M. (1998). *The Afrocentric idea* (Rev. & Expanded ed). Philadelphia: Temple University Press.

Au, K. H. (1979). Using the experience-text-relationship method with minority children. *Reading Teacher*, 32 (6), 677–679.

August, D., & Hakuta, K. (Eds.). (1997). *Improving schooling for language-minority children: A research agenda.* Washington, DC: National Academy Press.

Banks, C. A. M. (1996a). Intellectual leadership and African American challenges to meta-narratives. In J. A. Banks (Ed.), *Multicultural education, transformative knowledge, and action: Historical and contemporary perspectives* (pp. 46–63). New York: Teachers College Press.

Banks, C. A. M. (1996b). The intergroup education movement. In J. A. Banks (Ed.), *Multicultural education, transformative knowledge, and action* (pp. 251–277). New York: Teachers College Press.

Banks, C. A. M. (2001). Parents and teachers: Partners in school reform. In J. A. Banks & C. A. M. Banks (Eds.), *Multicultural education: Issues and perspectives* (4th ed., pp. 402–420). New York: Wiley.

Banks, J. A. (1988a). Approaches to multicultural curriculum reform. *Multicultural Leader,* 1(2), 1–3.

Banks, J. A. (1988b). Ethnicity, class, cognitive and motivational styles: Research and teaching implications. *The Journal of Negro Education,* 57, 452–466.

Banks, J. A. (1991a). Multicultural education: Its effects on students' racial and gender role attitudes. In J. P. Shaver (Ed.), *Handbook of research on social studies teaching and learning* (pp. 459–469). New York: Macmillan.

Banks, J. A. (1991b). Multicultural literacy and curriculum reform. *Educational Horizons,* 69 (3), 135–140.

Banks, J. A. (1993a). The canon debate, knowledge construction, and multicultural education. *Educational Researcher,* 22(5), 4–14.

Banks, J. A. (1993c). Multicultural education for young children: Racial and ethnic attitudes and their modification. In B. Spodek (Ed.), *Handbook of research on the education of young children* (pp. 236–250). New York: Macmillan.

Banks, J. A. (1995a). Multicultural education: Its effects on students' racial and gender role attitudes. In J. A. Banks & C. A. M. Banks (Eds.), *Handbook of research on multicultural education* (pp. 617–627). San Francisco: Jossey-Bass.

Banks, J. A. (1995b). Multicultural education: Historical development, dimensions, and practice. In J. A. Banks & C. A. M. Banks (Eds.), *Handbook of research on multicultural education* (pp. 3–24). San Francisco: Jossey-Bass.

Banks, J. A. (1996a). The canon debate, knowledge construction, and multicultural education. In J. A. Banks (Ed.), *Multicultural education, transformative knowledge, and action* (pp. 3–29). New York: Teachers College Press.

Banks, J. A. (1998). Multicultural education and the re-envisioning of America. Sachs Lecture presented at Teachers College, Columbia University, April 24, 1996.

Banks, J. A. (Ed.). (1996c). *Multicultural education, transformative knowledge, and action.* New York: Teachers College Press.

Banks, J. A. (1997a). *Educating citizens in a multicultural society.* New York: Teachers College Press.

Banks, J. A. (1997b). *Teaching strategies for ethnic studies* (6th ed.). Boston: Allyn and Bacon.

Banks, J. A. (1998). The lives and values of researchers: Implications for educating citizens in a multicultural society. *Educational Researcher,* 27(7), 4–17.

Banks, J. A. (2000). The social construction of difference and the quest for educational equality. In R. S. Brandt (Ed.), *Education in a new era* (pp. 21–45). Alexandria, VA: Association for Supervision and Curriculum Development.

Banks, J. A. (2001). *Cultural diversity and education: Foundations, curriculum and teaching* (4th ed.). Boston: Allyn and Bacon.

Banks, J. A., & Banks, C. A. M. (1983). The self-concept, locus of control, and racial attitudes of preschool and primary grade Black children who live in predominantly white suburban communities. Unpublished paper, University of Washington, Seattle.

Banks, J. A., & Banks, C. A. M. (Eds.). (1995). *Handbook of research on multicultural education.* San Francisco: Jossey-Bass.

Banks, J. A., & Banks, C. A. M., with Clegg, A. A., Jr. (1999). *Teaching strategies for the social studies* (5th ed.). White Plains, NY: Longman.

Banks, J. A., & Banks, C. A. M. (Eds.). (2001). *Multicultural education: Issues and perspectives* (4th ed.). New York: Wiley.

Banks, J. A., Cookson, P., Gay, G., Hawley, W. D., Irvine, J. J., Nieto, S., Schofield, J. W. & Stephan, W. G. (2001). *Diversity within unity: Essential principles for teaching and learning in a multicultural society.* Seattle: Center for Multicultural Education, University of Washington.

Banks, J. A., Cortés, C. E., Gay, G., Garcia, R. L., & Ochoa, A. (1992). *Curriculum guidelines for multicultural education* (Rev. ed.). Washington, DC: National Council for the Social Studies.

Banks, J. A., with Sebesta, S. L. (1982). *We Americans: Our history and people* (Vols. 1 and 2). Boston: Allyn and Bacon.

Bell, D. (1973). *The coming of the post-industrial society: A venture in social forecasting.* New York: Basic Books.

Berger, B. M. (1995). *An essay on culture: Symbolic structure and social structure.* Berkeley: The University of California Press.

Bernstein, R. (1994). *Dictatorship of virtue: Multiculturalism and the battle for America's future.* New York: A. A. Knopf.

Bigelow, B., & Peterson, B. (1998). *Rethinking Columbus: The next 500 years.* Milwaukee: Rethinking Schools.

Boykin, A. W. (1986). The triple quandary and the schooling of Afro-American children. In U. Neisser (Ed.)., *The school achievement of minority children: New perspectives* (pp. 57–92). Hillsdale, NJ: Lawrence Erlbaum.

Boykin, A. W. (2000). The talent development model of schooling: Placing students at promise for academic press. *Journal of Education for Students Placed At Risk,* 5 (1 & 2), 3–25.

Boykin, A. W., & Slavin, R. (Eds.). (2000). CRESPAR Findings (1994–1999): In memory of John H. Hollifield, Jr. *Journal of Education for Students Placed at Risk,* 5 (Special issue, 1 & 2), 3–208.

Branch, T. (1988). *Parting the waters: America in the King years 1954–63.* New York: Simon and Schuster.

Brimelow, P. (1995). *Alien nation.* New York: Random House.

Brinton, C. (1962). *The anatomy of revolution.* New York: Vintage.

Brodkin, K. (1998). *How the Jews became white folks and what that says about race in American.* New Brunswick, NJ: Rutgers University Press.

Brookover, W., Beady, C., Flood, P., Schweitzer, J., & Wisenbaker, J. (1979). *School social systems and student achievement: Schools can make a difference.* New York: Praeger.

Brookover, W. B., & Erickson, E. L. (1969). *Society, schools, and learning.* Boston: Allyn and Bacon.

Brophy, J., & Good, T. (1970). Teachers' communication of differential expectations for children's classroom performance: Some behavioral data. *Journal of Educational Psychology,* 61, 365–374.

Brown, J. W., Hughes, G. B. & Vance, P. L. (Eds.). (1999). Recruiting, preparing, and retaining qualified teachers to educate all of America's children in the 21st century. *The Journal of Negro Education,* 68 (3), Special issue.

Burns, G. M. (1978). *Leadership.* New York: Harper & Row.

Butler, J. E., & Walter, J. C. (Eds.). (1991). *Transforming the curriculum: Ethnic studies and women's studies.* Albany: State University of New York Press.

Carnochan, W. B. (1993). *The battleground of the curriculum: Liberal education and the American experience.* Stanford, CA: Stanford University Press.

Carter, R. T. (1995). *The influence of race and racial identity in psychotherapy.* New York: John Wiley and Sons.

Champagne, D. (1994). *Native America: Portrait of the peoples.* Detroit: Visible Ink.

Chavez, L. (1991). *Out of the barrio: Toward a new politics of Hispanic assimilation.* New York: Basic Books.

Chmelynski, C. (1990). Controversy attends schools with all-Black, all-male classes. *The Executive Educator,* 12, 16–18.

Clark, K. B., & Clark, M. P. (1939). The development of consciousness of self and the emergence of racial identification in Negro preschool children. *Journal of Social Psychology,* 10, 591–599.

Clark, K. B., & Clark, M. P. (1950). Emotional factors in racial identification and preference in Negro children. *Journal of Negro Education,* 19, 341–350.

Cochran-Smith, M. (2000). Blind vision: Unlearning racism in teacher education. *Harvard Educational Review,* 72(2), 157–190.

Code, L. (1991). *What can she know? Feminist theory and the construction of knowledge.* Ithaca, NY: Cornell University Press.

Cohen, E. (1994). *Designing groupwork: Strategies for heterogeneous classrooms* (2nd ed.). New York: Teachers College Press.

Cohen, E., & Lotan, R. A. (Eds.). (1997). *Working for equity in heterogeneous classrooms.* New York: Teachers College Press.

Cohen, E. G., & Roper, S. S. (1972). Modification of interracial interaction disability: An application of status characteristic theory. *American Sociological Review,* 37, 643–657.

Collins, P. H. (2000). *Black feminist thought: Knowledge, consciousness, and the politics of empowerment* (2nd ed.). New York: Routledge.

Comer, J. P. (1980). *School power: Implications of an intervention project.* New York: Free Press.

Comer, J. P. (1988). Educating poor minority children. *Scientific American,* 259(5), 42–48.

Comer, J. P., Haynes, N. M., Joyner, E. T., & Ben-Avie, M. (Eds.). (1996). *Rallying the whole village: The Comer process of reforming education.* New York: Teachers College Press.

Cose, E. (1993). *The rage of a privileged class.* New York: HarperCollins.

Crawford, J. (1989). *Bilingual education: History, politics, theory and practice.* Trenton, NJ: Crane.

Cremin, L. A. (1989). *Popular education and its discontents.* New York: Harper & Row.

Cross, W. E., Jr. (1991). *Shades of black: Diversity in African-American identity.* Philadelphia: Temple University Press.

Daley, S. (1990). Inspirational history draws academic fire. *The New York Times,* October 10, pp. B8 ff.

Daniels, R. (1988). *Asian America: Chinese and Japanese in the United States since 1850.* Seattle: University of Washington Press.

Darling-Hammond, L. (1997). *The right to learn: A blueprint for creating schools that work.* San Francisco: Jossey-Bass.

Delgado, R. (Ed.). (1995). *Critical race theory: The cutting edge.* Philadelphia: Temple University Press.

Delpit, L. D. (1988). The silenced dialogue: Power and pedagogy in educating other people's children. *Harvard Educational Review,* 58, 280–298.

Delpit, L. D. (1995). *Other people's children: Cultural conflict in the classroom.* New York: The New Press.

Delpit, L. D. (1997). Ebonics and culturally responsive instruction. *Rethinking Schools,* 12(1), 6–7.

Dershowitz, A. M. (1997). *The vanishing American Jew: In search of Jewish identity for the next century.* New York: Little Brown.

Diakiw, J. (1994). Growing up Ukrainian in Toronto. In C. E. James & A. Shadd (Eds.), *Talking about difference: Encounters in culture, language and identity* (pp. 49–55). Toronto, Canada: Between the Lines.

Diaz, C. F., Massialas, B. G., & Xanthopoulos, J. A. (1999). *Global perspectives for educators.* Boston: Allyn and Bacon.

Dickeman, M. (1973). Teaching cultural pluralism. In J. A. Banks (Ed.), *Teaching ethnic studies: Concepts and strategies* (pp. 5–25). Washington, DC: National Council for the Social Studies.

Dorris, M. (1992). *Morning girl.* New York: Hyperion Books for Children.

D'Souza, D. (1991). *Illiberal education: The politics of race and sex on campus.* New York: Free Press.

D'Souza, D. (1995). *The end of racism: Principles for a multicultural society.* New York: The Free Press.

Du Bois, W. E. B. (1935). *Black reconstruction.* Millwood, NY: Kraus-Thomson Organization Limited.

Edelman, M. W. (1992). *The measure of our success: A letter to my children and yours.* Boston: Beacon Press.

Edmonds, R. (1986). Characteristics of effective schools. In U. Neisser (Ed.), *The school achievement of minority children: New perspectives* (pp. 93–104). Hillsdale, NJ: Erlbaum.

Erickson, F. (2001). Culture in society and in educational practices. In J. A. Banks & C. A. M. Banks (Eds.), *Multicultural education: Issues and perspectives* (4th ed., pp.31–58). New York: John Wiley.

Feagin, J. R., & Sikes, M. P. (1994). *Living with racism: The Black middle-class experience.* Boston: Beacon Press.

Fine, M., Weis, L., Powell, L. C., & Wong, L. M. (Eds.). (1997). *Off white: Readings on race, power, and society.* New York: Routledge.

Finn, C. E., Jr. (1990). Why can't colleges convey our diverse culture's unifying themes? *The Chronicle of Higher Education,* 36, 40.

Fitzgerald, A. K., & Lauter, P. (1995). Multiculturalism and core curricula. In J. A. Banks & C. A. M. Banks (Eds.), *Handbook of research on multicultural education* (pp. 729–746). San Francisco: Jossey-Bass.

Foner, E. (1998). *The story of American freedom.* New York: Norton.

Ford, D. (1996). *Reversing underachievement among gifted Black students: Promising practices and programs.* New York: Teachers College Press.

Ford Foundation, Project on Social Welfare and the American Future. (1989). *The common good: Social welfare and the American future.* New York: Ford Foundation.

Fordham, S. (1996). *Blacked out: Dilemmas of race, identity, and success at Capital High.* Chicago: The University of Chicago Press.

Franklin, J. H. (1989). The moral legacy of the founding fathers. In J. H. Franklin, *Race and history: Selected essays 1938–1988* (pp. 153–179). Baton Rouge: Louisiana State University Press.

Franklin, J. H. (1995). Race and the Constitution in the nineteenth century. In J. H. Franklin & G. R. McNeil (Eds.), *African Americans and the living Constitution* (pp. 21–32). Washington, DC: Smithsonian Institution Press.

Franklin, J. H., & Moss, A. A., Jr. (1988). *From slavery to freedom: A history of Negro Americans* (6th ed.). New York: Knopf.

Freire, P. (1985). *The politics of education: Culture, power, and liberation.* New York: Bergin & Garvey.

Garcia, J. (1993). The changing image of ethnic groups in textbooks. *Phi Delta Kappan,* 75(1), 29–35.

Garcia, R. L. (1993). Prepublication review of the manuscript for 2nd edition of this book: *An introduction to multicultural education.*

Gardner, H. (1983). *Frames of mind: The theory of multiple intelligences.* New York: Basic Books.

Gay, G. (1995). Curriculum theory and multicultural education. In J. A. Banks & C. A. M. Banks (Eds.). *Handbook of research on multicultural education* (pp. 25–43). San Francisco: Jossey-Bass.

Gay, G. (2000). *Culturally responsive teaching: Theory, research and practice.* New York: Teachers College Press.

Geertz, C. (1995). *After the fact: Two countries, four decades, one anthropologist.* Cambridge, MA: Harvard University Press.

Gibbs, J. T. (Ed.). (1988). *Young, Black, and male in America: An endangered species.* Dover, MA: Auburn House Publishing.

Glazer, N. (1997). *We are all multiculturalists now.* Cambridge, MA: Harvard University Press.

Golden, R., McConnell, M., Mueller, P., Poppen, C., & Turkovich, M. (1991). *Dangerous memories: Invasion and resistance since 1492.* Chicago: The Chicago Religious Task Force on Central America.

Gonzales, M. G. (1999). *Mexicanos: A history of Mexicans in the United States.* Bloomington: Indiana University Press.

González, N., Moll, L., Flloyd-Tenery, M., Rivera, A., Rendón, P., Gonzales, R., & Amanti, C. (1993). *Teacher research on funds of knowledge: Learning from households*. Tucson, AZ: National Center for Research on Cultural Diversity and Second Language Learning, University of Arizona.

Goodman, M. E. (1952). *Race awareness in young children.* New York: Collier Books.

Gordon, M. M. (1964). *Assimilation in American life: The role of race, religion and national origins.* New York: Oxford University Press.

Gould, S. J. (1981). *The mismeasure of man.* New York: Norton.

Gould, S. J. (1994, November 28). Curveball. *The New Yorker,* 70(38), 139–149.

Graff, G. (1992). *Beyond the cultural wars: How teaching the conflicts can revitalize American education.* New York: Norton.

Graham, P. A. (1992). *S-O-S: Save our schools.* New York: Hill and Wang.

Grant, C. A., & Ladson-Billings, G. (Eds.). (1997). *Dictionary of multicultural education.* Phoenix, AZ: The Oryx Press.

Grant, C. A., & Sleeter, C. E. (2001). Race, class, gender, and disability in the classroom. In J. A. Banks & C. A. M. Banks (Eds.), *Multicultural education: Issues and perspectives* (4th ed., pp. 59–81). New York: Wiley.

Grant, C. A., & Tate, W. F. (1995). Multicultural education through the lens of the multicultural education literature. In J. A. Banks & C. A. M. Banks (Eds.), *Handbook of research on multicultural education* (pp. 145–166). San Francisco: Jossey-Bass.

Gray, P. (1991, July 8). Whose America? *Time,* 138, 13–17.

Greeno, J. G., Collins, A. M., & Resnick, L. (1996). Cognition and learning. In D. C. Berlinger & R. C. Calfee (Eds.), *Handbook of educational psychology* (pp. 15–46). New York: Macmillan.

Guggenheim, C. (1995). *The shadow of hate: A history of intolerance in America* [Videotape]. (Available from: Teaching Tolerance, 400 Washington Avenue, Montgomery, AL 36104.)

Gutiérrez, R. A. (1995). Historical and social science research on Mexican Americans. In J. A. Banks & C. A. M. Banks (Eds.), *Handbook of research on multicultural education* (pp. 203–222). San Francisco: Jossey-Bass.

Hale-Benson, J. E. (1986). *Black children: Their roots, cultures, and learning styles* (Rev. ed.). Baltimore: The Johns Hopkins University Press.

Hannaford, I. (1996). *Race: The history of an idea in the west.* Baltimore: The Johns Hopkins University Press.

Harding, S. (1991). *Whose knowledge? Whose science?: Thinking from women's lives.* Ithaca, NY: Cornell University Press.

Harding, S. (1998). *Is science multicultural? Postcolonialisms, feminisms, and epistemologies*. Bloomington: Indiana University Press.

Heath, S. B. (1983). *Ways with words: Language, life and work in communities and classrooms.* New York: Cambridge University Press.

Heath, S. B., & McLaughlin, M. W. (Eds.). (1993). *Identity & inner-city youth: Beyond ethnicity and gender.* New York: Teachers College Press.

Here they come, ready or not. (1986, May 14). *Education Week.* Special issue.

Herrnstein, R. J. (1971). IQ. *Atlantic Monthly, 228,* 43–64.

Herrnstein, R. J., & Murray, C. (1994). *The bell curve: Intelligence and class structure in American life.* New York: The Free Press.

Heubert, J. P., & Hauser, R. M. (Eds.). (1999). *High stakes: Testing for tracking, promotion, and graduation.* Washington, DC: National Academy Press.

Hidalgo, N. M., Bright, J. A., Siu, S-F, Swap, S. M., & Epstein, J. L. (1995). Research on families, schools, and communities: A multicultural perspective. In J. A. Banks & C. A. M. Banks (Eds.), *Handbook of research on multicultural education* (pp. 498–524). San Francisco: Jossey-Bass.

Hine, D. C., King, W., & Reed, L. (Eds.). (1995). *"We specialize in the wholly impossible": A reader in Black women's history.* Brooklyn, NY: Carlson Publishing.

Hirsch, E. D. (1987). *Cultural literacy: What every American needs to know.* Boston: Houghton Mifflin.

Hirschfelder, A. (Ed.). (1995). *Native heritage: Personal accounts by American Indians 1790 to the present.* New York: Macmillan.

Hodgkinson, H. (1991). Reform versus reality. *Phi Delta Kappan,* 73(1), 9–16.

Hodgkinson, H. L. (1985). *All one system: Demographics in education, kindergarten through graduate school.* Washington, DC: The Institute for Educational Leadership.

Hollins, E. R. (1996). *Culture in school learning: Revealing the deep meaning.* Mahwah, NJ: Lawrence Erlbaum.

Holmes, S. A. (2000, Dec 29). After standing up to be counted, Americans number 281, 421, 906. *The New York Times,* pp. A 1, ff. A 18.

Homans, G. C. (1967). *The nature of social science.* New York Harcourt Brace.

hooks, b. (1994). *Teaching to transgress: Education as the practice of freedom.* New York: Routledge.

Howard, G. (1996). Whites in multicultural education: Rethinking our role. In J. A. Banks (Ed.), *Multicultural education, transformative knowledge, and action* (pp. 323–334). New York: Teachers College Press.

Howard, G. (1999). *We can't teach what we don't know: White teachers, multiracial schools.* New York: Teachers College Press.

Hu-DeHart, E. (1995). Ethnic studies in U.S. higher education: History, development, and goals. In J. A. Banks & C. A. M. Banks (Eds.), *Handbook of research on multicultural education* (pp. 696–707). San Francisco: Jossey-Bass.

Ignatiev, I. (1995). *How the Irish became White.* New York: Routledge.

Indianapolis Public Schools. (1996, November). *Resolution No. 7397: Indianapolis Public Schools multicultural education.* Indianapolis: Author.

Irvine, J. J. (1990). *Black students and school failure: Policies, practices, and prescriptions.* New York: Praeger.

Irvine, J. J., & York, D. E. (1995). Learning styles and culturally diverse students: A literature review. In J. A. Banks & C. A. McGee Banks (Eds.), *Handbook of research on multicultural education* (pp. 484–497). San Francisco: Jossey-Bass.

Jacobson, M. F. (1998). *Whiteness of a different color: European immigrants and the alchemy of race.* Cambridge, MA: Harvard University Press.

Jacoby, S. (2000). *Half-Jew: A daughter's search for her family's buried past.* New York: Scribners.

Jane, L. C. (1989). *The journal of Christopher Columbus.* New York: Bonanza Books.

Jensen, A. R. (1969). How much can we boost IQ and scholastic achievement? *Harvard Educational Review,* 39, 1–123.

Johnson, W. B., & Packer, A. B. (1987). *Workforce 2000: Work and workers for the 21st century.* Washington, D.C.: U.S. Government Printing Office.

Jones, J. (1985). *Labor of love, labor of sorrow: Black women, work, and the family from slavery to the present.* New York: Basic Books.

Jordan, W. (1968). *White over Black: American attitudes toward the Negro, 1550–1812.* Chapel Hill: University of North Carolina Press.

Josephy, A. M., Jr. (1992). *America in 1492: The world of the Indian peoples before the arrival of Columbus.* New York: Knopf.

Kammen, M. (1997). *In the past lane: Historical perspectives on American culture.* New York: Oxford University Press.

Katz, P. A., & Zalk, S. R. (1978). Modification of children's racial attitudes. *Developmental Psychology,* 14, 447–461.

Keen, B. (Trans.). (1959). *The life of the Admiral Christopher Columbus by his son Ferdinand.* New Brunswick, NJ: Rutgers University Press.

King, M. L. (1987). Selected by C. S. King. *The words of Martin Luther King, Jr.* New York: Newmarket Press.

Kohlberg, L., & Turiel, E. (1971). Moral development and moral education. In G. S. Lesser (Ed.), *Psychology and educational practice* (pp. 410–465). Glenview, IL: Scott, Foresman.

Kohn, A. (2000). *The case against standardized testing.* Portsmouth, NH: Heinemann.

Kozol, J. (1991). *Savage inequalities: Children in America's schools.* New York: Crown.

Kozulin, A. (Ed.). (1986). *Thought and language: Lev Vygotsky.* Cambridge, MA: The MIT Press.

Kymlicka, W. (1995). *Multicultural citizenship: A liberal theory of minority rights.* New York: Oxford University Press.

Ladson-Billings, G. (1990). Like lightning in a bottle: Attempting to capture the pedagogical excellence of successful teachers of Black students. *International Journal of Qualitative Studies in Education,* 3, 335–344.

Ladson-Billings, G. (1994). *The dreamkeepers: Successful teachers of African American children.* San Francisco: Jossey-Bass.

Ladson-Billings, G. (1999). Preparing teachers for diversity: Historical perspectives, current trends, and future directions. In L. Darling-Hammond & G. Sykes (Eds.), *Teaching as the learning profession* (pp. 86–123). San Francisco: Jossey-Bass.

Ladson-Billings, G. (2001). *Crossing over to Cannan: The journey of new teachers in diverse classrooms.* San Francisco: Jossey-Bass.

Lasker, B. (1929). *Race attitudes in children.* New York: Holt.

Lee, C. D. (1993). *Signifying as a scaffold for literary interpretation: The pedagogical implications of an African American discourse genre.* Urbana, IL: National Council of Teachers of English.

Leo, J. (2000). *Incorrect thoughts: Notes on our wayward culture.* Piscataway, NJ: Transaction.

Lerner, G. (1997). *Why history matters: Life and thought.* New York: Oxford University Press.

Levine, D. U., & Lezotte, L. W. (1995). Effective schools research. In J. A. Banks & C. A. M. Banks (Eds.), *Handbook of research on multicultural education* (pp. 525–547). San Francisco: Jossey Bass

Lightfoot, S. L. (1988). *Balm in Gilead: Journey of a healer.* Reading, MA: Addison Wesley.

Limerick, P. N. (1987). *The legacy of conquest: The unbroken past of the American west.* New York: Norton.

Limerick, P. N. (2000). *Something in the social: Legacies and reckonings in the new west.* New York: Norton.

Litcher, J. H., & Johnson, D. W. (1969). Changes in attitudes toward Negroes of White elementary school students after use of multiethnic readers. *Journal of Educational Psychology, 60,* 148–152.

Litcher, J. H., Johnson, D. W., & Ryan, F. L. (1973). Use of pictures of multiethnic interaction to change attitudes of White elementary school students toward Blacks. *Psychological Reports, 33,* 367–372.

Lomawaima, K. T. (1995). Educating Native Americans. In J. A. Banks & C. A. M. Banks (Eds.), *Handbook of research on multicultural education* (pp. 331–347). San Francisco: Jossey-Bass.

Marshall, G. (1994). *The concise Oxford dictionary of sociology.* New York: Oxford University Press.

Mehan, H., Villanueva, I., Hubbard, L., & Lintz, A. (1996). *Constructing school success: The consequences of untracking low-achieving students.* New York: Cambridge University Press.

McConnell, S., & Breindel, E. (1990, January 8 and 15). Head to come. *The New Republic,* pp. 19–21.

McGoldrick, M., Giordano, J., & Pearce, J. K. (Eds.). (1996). *Ethnicity and family therapy* (2nd ed.). New York: The Guilford Press.

McIntosh, P. (1997). White privilege: Unpacking the invisible knapsack. In V. Cyrus (Ed.), *Experiencing race, class, and gender* (2nd ed., pp. 194–198). Mountain View, CA: Mayfield Publishing Company.

McLaren, P. (1997). *Revolutionary multiculturalism: Pedagogies of dissent for the new millennium.* Boulder, CO: Westview Press.

McNeil, L. M. (2000). *Contradictions of school reform: Educational costs of standardized testing.* New York: Routledge.

Meier, D. (Ed.). (2000). *Will standards save public education?* Boston: Beacon Press.

Mercer, J. R. (1989). Alternative paradigms for assessment in a pluralistic society. In J. A. Banks & C. A. M. Banks (Eds.), *Multicultural education: Issues and perspectives* (1st ed., pp. 289–304). Boston: Allyn and Bacon.

Minami, M., & Kennedy, B. P. (Eds.). (1992). *Language issues in literacy and bilingual/multicultural education.* Cambridge, MA: Harvard Educational Review Reprint Series #22.

Minnich, E. K. (1990). *Transforming knowledge.* Philadelphia: Temple University Press.

Morgan, E. S. (1975). *American slavery, American freedom: The ordeal of colonial Virginia.* New York: Norton.

Morison, S. E. (1974). *The European discovery of America: The southern voyages 1492–1616*. New York: Oxford University Press.

Morrison, T. (1992). *Playing in the dark: Whiteness and the literary imagination.* Cambridge, MA: Harvard University Press.

Muir, K. (1990). *Eyes on The Prize: A review.* Paper submitted to J. A. Banks as partial requirement for the course EDUC 423, Educating diverse groups. Seattle, University of Washington.

Muzzey, D. S. (1915). *Readings in American history.* Boston: Ginn.

Myrdal, G. (with Sterner, R., & Rose, A.). (1944). *An American dilemma: The Negro problem and modern democracy.* New York: Harper & Row.

Nash, G. B. (1999). *Forbidden love: The secret history of mixed-race America.* New York: Henry Holt.

National Center for Education Statistics. (2001). *Statistics in brief.* Washington, DC: U. S. Department of Education, Office of Educational Research and Improvement.

National Council for the Accreditation of Teacher Education. (1997). *Standards for procedures & policies for the accreditation of professional education units.* Washington, DC: Author.

National Geographic Society. (1991, October). America before Columbus. *National Geographic,* 180(4), 1–124 [Special issue].

Nebraska Legislature. (1992, January 8). *Legislature Bill 922, Final Reading. Ninety-Second Legislature, Second Session.* Lincoln, NE: Author.

New York (City) Board of Education. (1989). *Statement of policy on multicultural education and promotion of positive intergroup relations.* New York: Author.

Nieto, S. (1999). *The light in their eyes: Creating multicultural learning communities.* New York. Teachers College Press.

Nieto, S. (Ed.). (2000). *Puerto Rican students in U. S. schools.* Mahwah, NJ: Lawrence Erlbaum.

Oakes, J. (1992). Can tracking research inform practice? Technical, normative, and political considerations. *Educational Researcher,* 21(4), 12–21.

Okihiro, G. (1994). *Margins and mainstreams: Asians in American history and culture.* Seattle: University of Washington Press.

Oliver, D. W., & Shaver, J. P. (1966). *Teaching public issues in the high school.* Boston: Houghton Mifflin.

Olsen, F. (1974). *On the trail of the Arawaks.* Norman: University of Oklahoma Press.

Olson, J. S., & Olson, J. E. (1995). *Cuban Americans: From trauma to triumph.* New York: Twayne Publishers.

Omi, M., & Winant, H. (1994). *Racial formation in the United States* (2nd ed.). New York: Routledge.

Orwell, G. (1946). *Animal farm.* New York: Harcourt Brace.

Ovando, C. J., & Collier, V. P. (1998). *Bilingual and ESL classrooms: Teaching in multicultural contexts* (2nd ed.). New York: McGraw-Hill.

Pallas, A. M., Natriello, G., & McDill, E. L. (1989). The changing nature of the disadvantaged population: Current dimensions and future trends. *Educational Researcher,* 18, 16–22.

Parekh, B. (1986). The concept of multicultural education. In S. Modgil, G. K. Verma, K. Mallick, & C. Modgil (Eds.), *Multicultural education: The interminable debate* (pp. 19–31). Philadelphia: Falmer Press.

Patterson, O. (1977). *Ethnic chauvinism: The reactionary impulse.* New York: Stein and Day.

Perry, T., & Delpit, L. (Eds.). (1998). *The real Ebonics debate: Power, language, and the education of African-American children.* Boston: Beacon Press.

Peters, W. (1987). *A class divided: Then and now* (Expanded Ed.). New Haven, CT: Yale University Press.

Philips, S. U. (1983). *The invisible culture: Communication in a classroom and community on the Warm Spring Indian Reservation.* New York: Longman.

Phillips, K. (1990). *The politics of rich and poor.* New York: Random House.

Ponce de Leon, J. (1992). The Native American response to the Columbus quincentenary. *Multicultural Review,* 1, 20–22.

Ponterotto, J. G., Casas, J. M., Suzuki, L. A., & Alexander, C. M. (Eds.). (1995). *Handbook of multicultural counseling.* Thousand Oaks, CA: Sage.

Pratt, R., & Rittenhouse, G. (Eds.).(1998). *The condition of education, 1998.* Washington, DC: U. S. Government Printing Office.

Quality Education for Minorities Project. (1990). *Education that works: An action plan for the education of minorities.* Cambridge, MA: Massachusetts Institute of Technology.

Ramírez, M. III, & Castañeda, A. (1974). *Cultural democracy, bicognitive development, and education.* New York: Academic Press.

Ravitch, D. (1990a). Diversity and democracy: Multicultural education in America. *American Educator,* 14, 16–20 ff. 46–48.

Ravitch, D. (1990b). Multiculturalism yes, particularism no. *The Chronicle of Higher Education,* A44.

Ravitch D., & Finn, C. E., Jr. (1987). *What do our 17-year-olds know? A report on the first national assessment of history and literature.* New York: Harper & Row.

Reschly, D. J. (1988). Minority MMR overrepresentation and special education reform. *Exceptional Children,* 54, 316–323.

Richman, L. S. (1990, April 9). The coming world labor shortage. *Fortune,* 70–77.

Rodriguez, C. E. (1989). *Puerto Ricans born in the U.S. A.* Boston: Unwin Hyman.

Rodriguez, R. (1982). *Hunger of memory: The education of Richard Rodriguez.* Boston: David R. Godine Publisher.

Root, M. P. P. (1996). *The multiracial experience: Racial borders as the new frontier.* Thousand Oaks, CA: Sage.

Rosenstein, J. (Writer, Producer, Ed.). (1997). *In whose honor? American Indian mascots in sports* [Videotape]. Available from New Day Films, 22D Hollywood Avenue, Ho-ho-kus, NJ 07423; (888) 367-9154.

Rosenthal, R., & Jacobson, L. (1968). *Pygmalion in the classroom: Teacher expectations and pupils' intellectual development.* New York: Holt, Rinehart & Winston.

Rouse, I. (1992). *The Tainos: Rise and decline of the people who greeted Columbus.* New Haven, CT: Yale University Press.

Sapon-Shevin, M. (1994). *Playing favorites: Gifted education and the disruption of community.* Albany: State University of New York Press.

Schlesinger, A. (1991). *The disuniting of America: Reflections on a multicultural society.* Knoxville, TN: Whittle Direct Books.

Schofield, J. W. (2001). The colorblind perspective in school: Causes and consequences. In J. A. Banks & C. A M. Banks (Eds.), *Multicultural education: Issues and perspectives* (4th ed., pp. 327–352). New York: John Wiley.

Selden, S. (1999). *Inheriting shame: The story of eugenics and racism in America.* New York: Teachers College Press.

Shade, B. J., Kelly, C., & Oberg, M. (1997). *Creating culturally responsive classrooms.* Washington, DC: American Psychological Association.

Shirts, G. (1969). *Starpower.* LaJolla, CA: Western Behavioral Science Institute.

Sirkin, G. (1990, January 18). The multiculturalists strike again. *The Wall Street Journal,* p. A14.

Slavin, R. E. (1983). *Cooperative learning.* New York: Longman.

Slavin, R. E. (1995). Cooperative learning and intergroup relations. In J. A. Banks & C. A. M. Banks (Eds.), *Handbook of research on multicultural education* (pp. 628–634). San Francisco: Jossey-Bass.

Sleeter, C. E. (1995). An analysis of the critiques of multicultural education. In J. A. Banks & C. A. M. Banks (Eds.), *Handbook of research on multicultural education* (pp. 81–94). San Francisco: Jossey-Bass.

Sleeter, C. E., & Grant, C. A. (1997). An analysis of multicultural education in the United States. *Harvard Educational Review, 7,* 421–444.

Smitherman, G. (2000). *Talkin that talk: Language, culture, and education in African America.* New York: Routledge.

Snipp, C. M. (1989). *American Indians: The first of this land.* New York: Russell Sage Foundation.

Spencer, M. B. (1982). Personal and group identity of Black children: An alternative synthesis. *Genetic Psychology Monographs,* 106, 59–84.

Spencer, M. B. (1984). Black children's race awareness, racial attitudes, and self-concept: A reinterpretation. *Journal of Child Psychology and Psychiatry,* 25, 433–441.

Staff of *Fortune.* (1990, March 26). An American vision for the 1990s. *Fortune,* pp. 14, 16.

Stahl, R. J., & VanSickle, R. L. (Eds.). (1992). *Cooperative learning in the social studies classroom.* Bulletin No. 87. Washington, DC: National Council for the Social Studies.

Stannard, D. E. (1992). *American holocaust: Columbus and the conquest of the new world.* New York: Oxford University Press.

Steele, C. M., & Aronson, J. (1995). Stereotype threat and the intellectual test performance of African Americans. *Journal of Personality and Social Psychology,* 69 (5), 797–812.

Stephan, W. G. (1999). *Reducing prejudice and stereotyping in schools.* New York: Teachers College Press.

Sue, D. W. (1995). Toward a theory of multicultural counseling and therapy. In J. A. Banks & C. A. M. Banks (Eds.). *Handbook of research on multicultural education* (pp. 647–659). San Francisco: Jossey-Bass.

Taba, H., Brady, E., & Robinson, J. (1952). *Intergroup education in public schools.* Washington, DC: American Council on Education.

Taba, H., Durkin, M. C., Fraenkel, J. & McNaughton, A. N. (1971). *A teacher's handbook to elementary social studies: An inductive approach* (2nd ed.). Reading, MA: Addison-Wesley.

Tajfel, H. (1970). Experiments in intergroup discrimination. *Scientific American,* 223(5), 96–102.

Tajfel, H., & Turner, J. C. (1986). The social identity theory of intergroup behavior. In S. Worchel & W. G. Austin (Eds.), *Psychology of intergroup relations* (2nd ed., pp. 7–24). Chicago: Nelson Hall Publishers.

Takaki, R. (1989). *Strangers from a different shore: A history of Asian Americans.* Boston: Little, Brown.

Tharp, R. G. (1982). The effective instruction of comprehension: Results and description of the Kamehameha Early Education Program. *Reading Research Quarterly,* 17(4), 503–527.

Tharp, R. G., Estrada, P., Dalton, S. S., &: Yamauchi, L. A. (2000). *Teaching transformed: Achieving excellence, fairness, inclusion, and harmony.* Boulder, CO: Westview.

Todorov, T. (1984). *The conquest of America: The question of the other.* New York: Harper and Row.

Toffler, A. (1980) *The third wave.* New York: William Morrow.

Trager, H. G., & Yarrow, M. R. (1952). *They learn what they live: Prejudice in young children.* New York: Harper and Brothers.

Turner, F. J. (1894/1989). The significance of the frontier in American history. In C. A. Milner II (Ed.), *Major problems in the history of the American West* (pp. 2–21). Lexington, MA: Heath.

USA Today. (1995, July 25). p. 1A.

U.S. Census Bureau. (1992, July). *We asked…you told us: Race.* Washington, DC: U.S. Government Printing Office.

U.S. Census Bureau. (1992, November). *We asked…you told us: Hispanic origin.* Washington, DC: U.S. Government Printing Office.

U.S. Census Bureau. (1994). *Statistical abstract of the United States: 1994* (114th ed.). Washington, DC: U.S. Government Printing Office.

U.S. Census Bureau. (1998). *Statistical abstract of the United States* (118th ed.). Washington, DC: U.S. Government Printing Office.

U.S. Census Bureau (2000). *Statistical Abstract of the United States: 2000* (120th ed.). Washington, DC: U.S. Government Printing Office.

U.S. Department of Education, Office for Civil Rights. (1996). *State summaries of National Center for Education Statistics, common core of data survey.* Washington, DC: U.S. Government Printing Office.

U.S. Department of Labor. (2001). Bureau of Labor Statistics (on-line: http:///www.bls.gov/news.release/ecopro.nr0.htm).

Valenzuela, A. (1999). *Substractive schooling: U.S.-Mexican youth and the politics of caring.* Albany: State University of New York Press.

Van Sertima, I. V. (Ed.). (1984). *Black women in antiquity.* New Brunswick, NJ: Transaction Books.

Vogt, L. A., Jordan, C., & Tharp, R. G. (1987). Explaining school failure, producing school success: Two cases. *Anthropology & Education Quarterly,* 18, 277–286.

Weatherford, J. (1992). *Native roots: How the Indians enriched America.* New York: Fawcett Columbine.

Wells, A. S., Hirshberg, D., Lipton, M., & Oaks, J. (1995). Bounding the case within its context: A constructivist approach to studying detracking reform. *Educational Researcher,* 24(5), 18–24.

White, J. L., & Parham, T. A. (1990). *The psychology of Blacks: An African-American perspective* (2nd ed.) Englewood Cliffs, NJ: Prentice-Hall.

White, R. (1991). *"It's your misfortune and none of my own." A new history of the American west.* Norman: University of Oklahoma Press.

Williams, F. (Ed.). (1970). *Language and poverty: Perspectives on a theme.* Chicago: Markham.

Williams, J. E., & Edwards, C. D. (1969). An exploratory study of the modification of color and racial concept attitudes in preschool children. *Child Development,* 40, 737–750.

Williams, J. E., & Morland, J. K. (1976). *Race, color and the young child.* Chapel Hill: University of North Carolina Press.

Wilson, W. J. (1996). *When work disappears: The world of the new urban poor.* New York: Knopf.

Wright, M. A. (1998). *I'm chocolate, your're vanilla: Raising healthy black and biracial children in a race-conscious world.* San Francisco: Jossey-Bass.

Zigmond, N. (Ed.). (1992). Issues in the education of African-American youth in special education settings. *Exceptional Children,* 59, 99–176 (Special issue).

Zinn, H. (2001). *Howard Zinn on history.* New York: Seven Stories Press.

Zúñiga, Z., & Nagda, B. (1993). Dialogue groups: An innovative approach to multicultural learning. In D. Schoem, L. Frankel, X. Zúñiga, & E. Lewis (Eds.), *Multicultural teaching in the university.* Westport, CT: Praeger.

INDEX

This page constitutes a continuation of the copyright page.

Credits: James A. Banks, "Approaches to Multicultural Curriculum Reform." *Multicultural Leader,* Vol. 1, No. 2 (Spring, 1988), pp. 1–3; James A. Banks, "Multicultural Education: Development, Dimensions, and Challenges." *Phi Delta Kappan,* Vol. 75, No. 1 (Sept. 1993), pp. 22–28; James A. Banks, "Multicultural Literacy and Curriculum Reform." *Educational Horizons,* Vol. 69, No. 3 (Spring, 1991), pp. 135–140; James A. Banks, *Multiethnic Education: Practices and Promises.* Bloomington, IN: Phi Delta Kappa Educational Foundation, 1977. Revised with a new bibliography, 1988; James A. Banks, "Reducing Prejudice in Children: Guidelines from Research." *Social Studies and the Young Learner,* Vol. 5, No. 2 (Nov./Dec. 1992), pp. 3–5; James A. Banks, *Preparing Teachers and Administrators in a Multicultural Society.* Austin, TX: Southwest Educational Development Laboratory, 1990. Revised with permission; "Citizenship Education and Diversity: Implications for Teacher Education," *Journal of Teacher Education,* Vol. 52 (No. 1), pp. 5–16. Copyright © 2001 by Sage Publications, Inc. Reprinted by permission of Sage Publications, Inc.; "Essential Principles for Teaching and Learning in a Multicultural Society." from J. A. Banks, P. Cookson, G. Gay, W. D. Hawley, J. J. Irvine, S. Nieto, J. W. Schofield, & W. G. Stephan (2001), *Diversity Within Unity: Essential Principles for Teaching and Learning in a Multicultural Society.* Seattle: Center for Multicultural Education, University of Washington. Reprinted with permission of the Center for Multicultural Education. James A. Banks with Sam L. Sebesta, *We Americans: Our History and People,* Vol. 1. Boston: Allyn & Bacon, 1982, pp. 35–43; From *The Journal of Christopher Columbus* by Anthony Blond. Copyright © 1960 by Clarkson N. Potter, Inc. Reprinted by permission of Crown Publishers, Inc.; *Legislative Bill 922.* Legislature of Nebraska 92nd Legislature, Second Session, Final Reading; Adapted from Margaret Smith Crocco, "Interview with James A. Banks." *Social Science Record,* Vol. 33, No. 2 (Fall 1996), pp. 27–34; Nebraska Department of Education, *Rule 16,* Approval of School District Multicultural Education Programs, Title 92, Nebraska Administrative Code, Chapter 16, Effective October 11, 1993.